COUNTERFEIT GIRL

PETER MILLIGAN　**RUFUS DAYGLO**　**DOM REGAN**

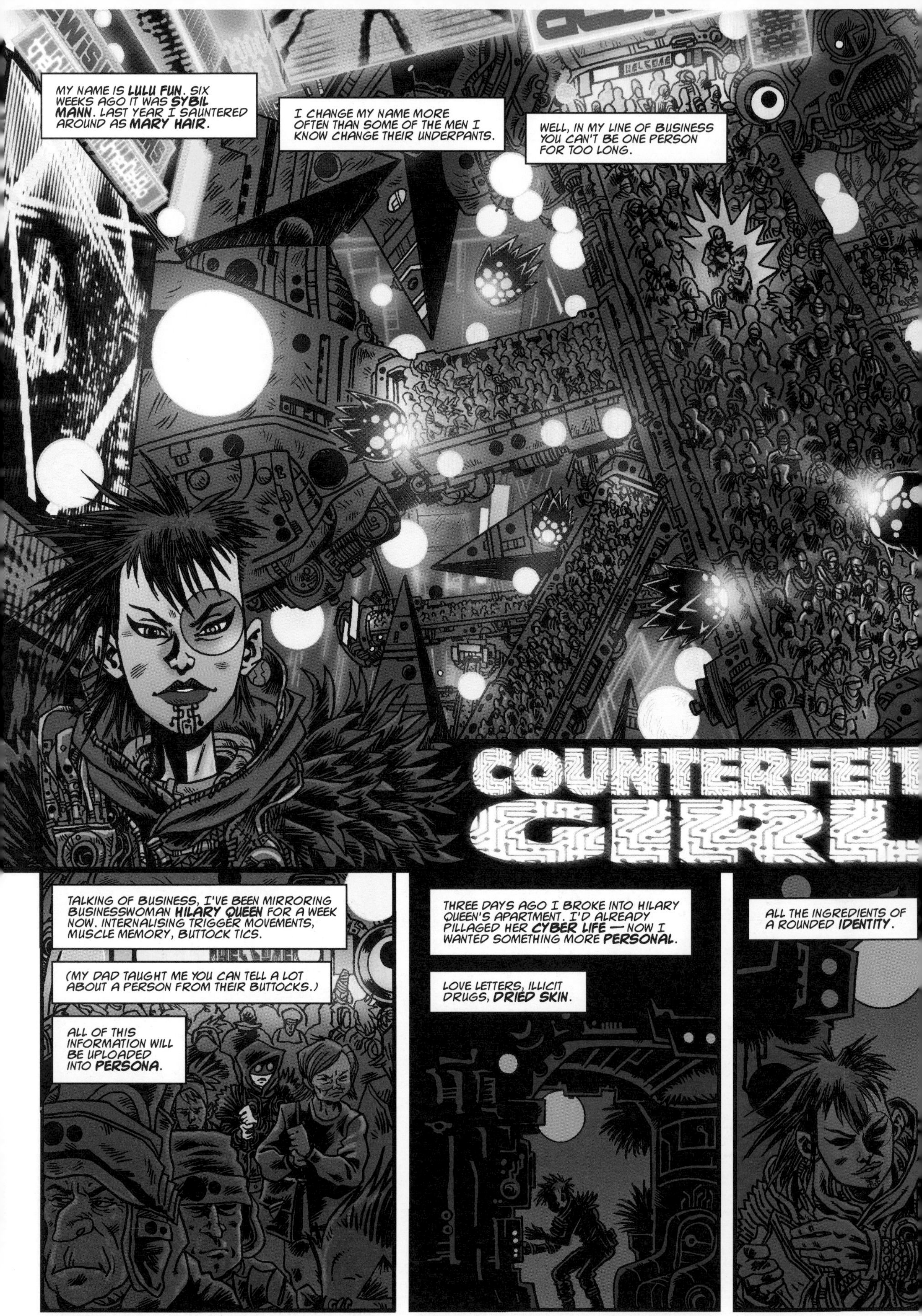
MY NAME IS **LULU FUN**. SIX WEEKS AGO IT WAS **SYBIL MANN**. LAST YEAR I SAUNTERED AROUND AS **MARY HAIR**.
I CHANGE MY NAME MORE OFTEN THAN SOME OF THE MEN I KNOW CHANGE THEIR UNDERPANTS.
WELL, IN MY LINE OF BUSINESS YOU CAN'T BE ONE PERSON FOR TOO LONG.
COUNTERFEIT GIRL
TALKING OF BUSINESS, I'VE BEEN MIRRORING BUSINESSWOMAN **HILARY QUEEN** FOR A WEEK NOW. INTERNALISING TRIGGER MOVEMENTS, MUSCLE MEMORY, BUTTOCK TICS.
(MY DAD TAUGHT ME YOU CAN TELL A LOT ABOUT A PERSON FROM THEIR BUTTOCKS.)
ALL OF THIS INFORMATION WILL BE UPLOADED INTO **PERSONA**.
THREE DAYS AGO I BROKE INTO HILARY QUEEN'S APARTMENT. I'D ALREADY PILLAGED HER **CYBER LIFE** — NOW I WANTED SOMETHING MORE **PERSONAL**.
LOVE LETTERS, ILLICIT DRUGS, **DRIED SKIN**.
ALL THE INGREDIENTS OF A ROUNDED **IDENTITY**.

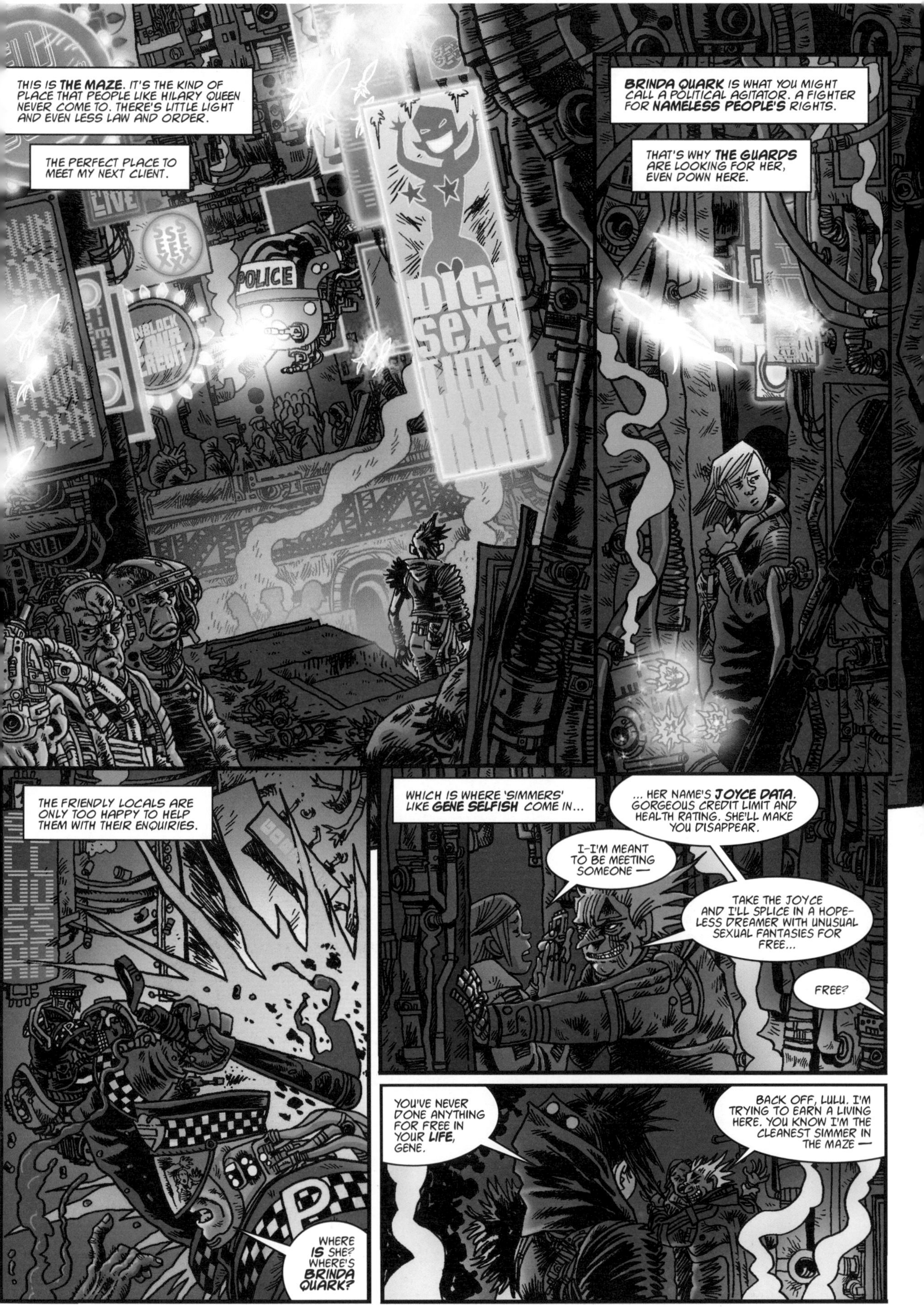
THIS IS **THE MAZE**. IT'S THE KIND OF PLACE THAT PEOPLE LIKE HILARY QUEEN NEVER COME TO. THERE'S LITTLE LIGHT AND EVEN LESS LAW AND ORDER.
THE PERFECT PLACE TO MEET MY NEXT CLIENT.
POLICE
BRINDA QUARK IS WHAT YOU MIGHT CALL A POLITICAL AGITATOR. A FIGHTER FOR **NAMELESS PEOPLE'S** RIGHTS.
THAT'S WHY **THE GUARDS** ARE LOOKING FOR HER, EVEN DOWN HERE.
THE FRIENDLY LOCALS ARE ONLY TOO HAPPY TO HELP THEM WITH THEIR ENQUIRIES.
WHERE **IS** SHE? WHERE'S **BRINDA QUARK?**
WHICH IS WHERE 'SIMMERS' LIKE **GENE SELFISH** COME IN...
... HER NAME'S **JOYCE DATA**. GORGEOUS CREDIT LIMIT AND HEALTH RATING. SHE'LL MAKE YOU DISAPPEAR.
I-I'M MEANT TO BE MEETING SOMEONE —
TAKE THE JOYCE AND I'LL SPLICE IN A HOPE-LESS DREAMER WITH UNUSUAL SEXUAL FANTASIES FOR FREE...
FREE?
YOU'VE NEVER DONE ANYTHING FOR FREE IN YOUR **LIFE**, GENE.
BACK OFF, LULU. I'M TRYING TO EARN A LIVING HERE. YOU KNOW I'M THE CLEANEST SIMMER IN THE MAZE —

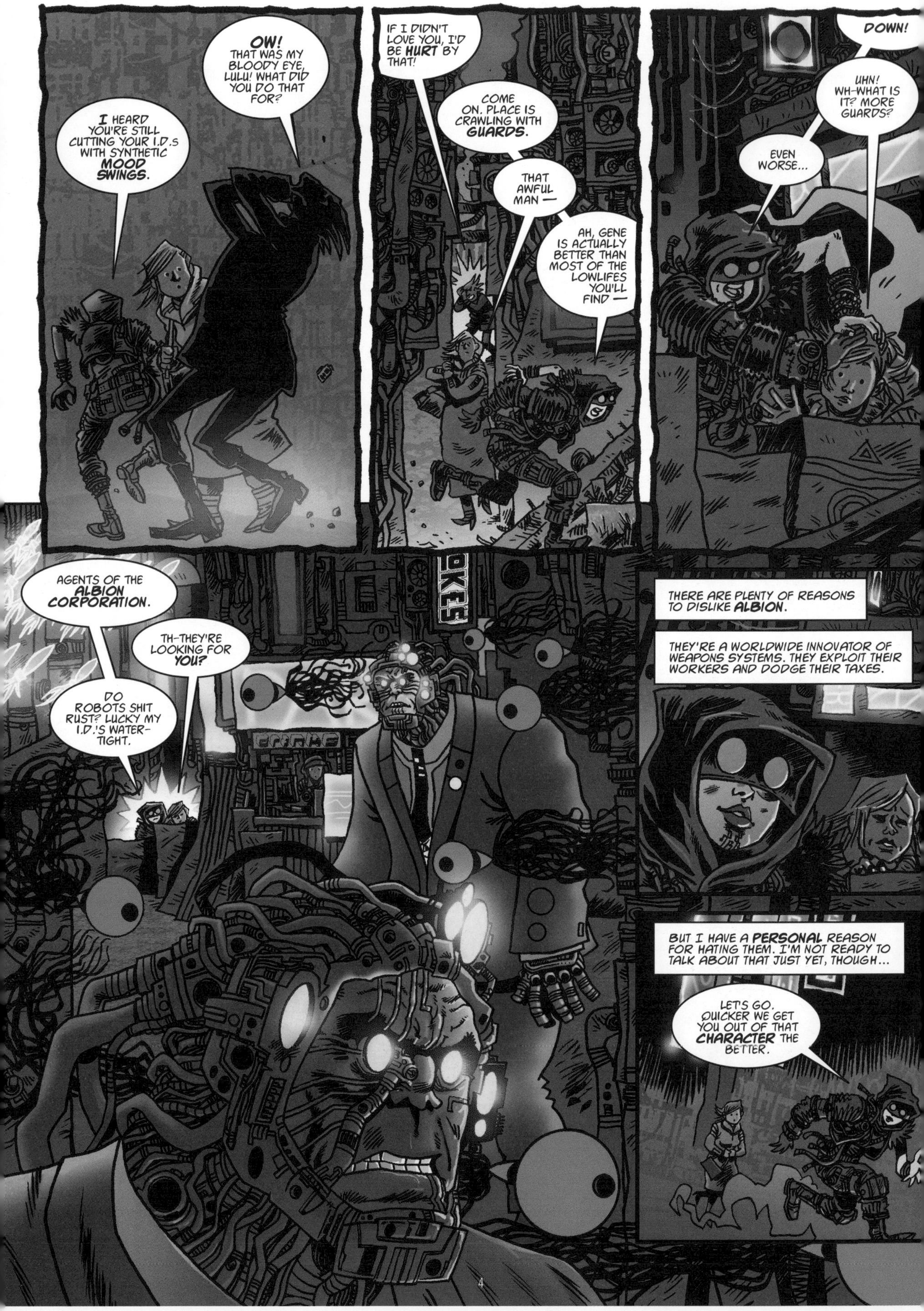
I HEARD YOU'RE STILL CUTTING YOUR I.D.S WITH SYNTHETIC MOOD SWINGS.
OW! THAT WAS MY BLOODY EYE, LULU! WHAT DID YOU DO THAT FOR?
IF I DIDN'T LOVE YOU, I'D BE HURT BY THAT!
COME ON. PLACE IS CRAWLING WITH GUARDS.
THAT AWFUL MAN —
AH, GENE IS ACTUALLY BETTER THAN MOST OF THE LOWLIFES YOU'LL FIND —
DOWN!
UHN! WH–WHAT IS IT? MORE GUARDS?
EVEN WORSE...
AGENTS OF THE ALBION CORPORATION.
TH-THEY'RE LOOKING FOR YOU?
DO ROBOTS SHIT RUST? LUCKY MY I.D.'S WATER-TIGHT.
THERE ARE PLENTY OF REASONS TO DISLIKE ALBION.
THEY'RE A WORLDWIDE INNOVATOR OF WEAPONS SYSTEMS. THEY EXPLOIT THEIR WORKERS AND DODGE THEIR TAXES.
BUT I HAVE A PERSONAL REASON FOR HATING THEM. I'M NOT READY TO TALK ABOUT THAT JUST YET, THOUGH...
LET'S GO. QUICKER WE GET YOU OUT OF THAT CHARACTER THE BETTER.

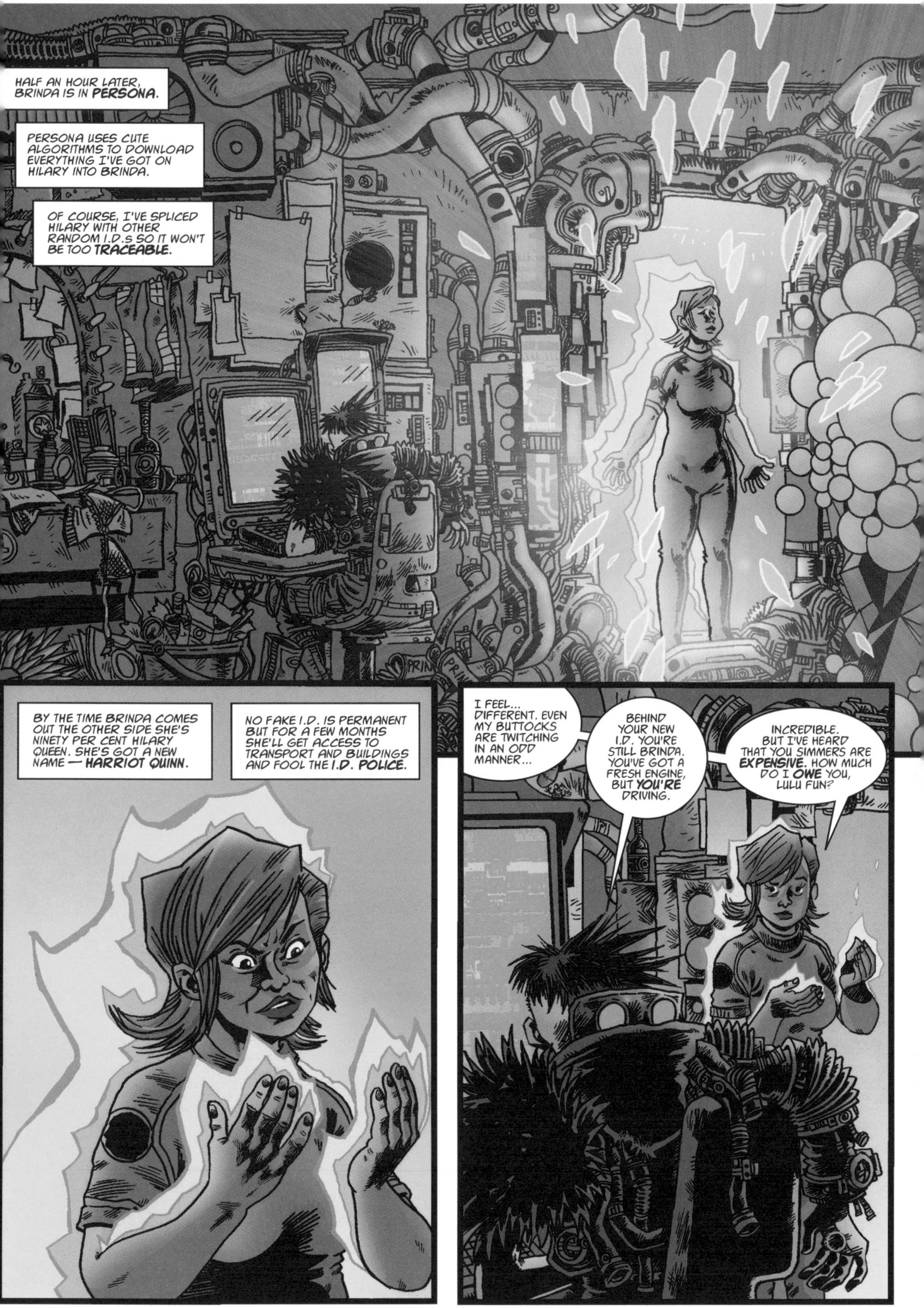
HALF AN HOUR LATER, BRINDA IS IN **PERSONA**.
PERSONA USES CUTE ALGORITHMS TO DOWNLOAD EVERYTHING I'VE GOT ON HILARY INTO BRINDA.
OF COURSE, I'VE SPLICED HILARY WITH OTHER RANDOM I.D.s SO IT WON'T BE TOO **TRACEABLE**.
BY THE TIME BRINDA COMES OUT THE OTHER SIDE SHE'S NINETY PER CENT HILARY QUEEN. SHE'S GOT A NEW NAME — **HARRIOT QUINN**.
NO FAKE I.D. IS PERMANENT BUT FOR A FEW MONTHS SHE'LL GET ACCESS TO TRANSPORT AND BUILDINGS AND FOOL THE **I.D. POLICE**.
I FEEL... DIFFERENT. EVEN MY BUTTOCKS ARE TWITCHING IN AN ODD MANNER...
BEHIND YOUR NEW I.D. YOU'RE STILL BRINDA. YOU'VE GOT A FRESH ENGINE, BUT **YOU'RE** DRIVING.
INCREDIBLE. BUT I'VE HEARD THAT YOU SIMMERS ARE **EXPENSIVE**. HOW MUCH DO I **OWE** YOU, LULU FUN?

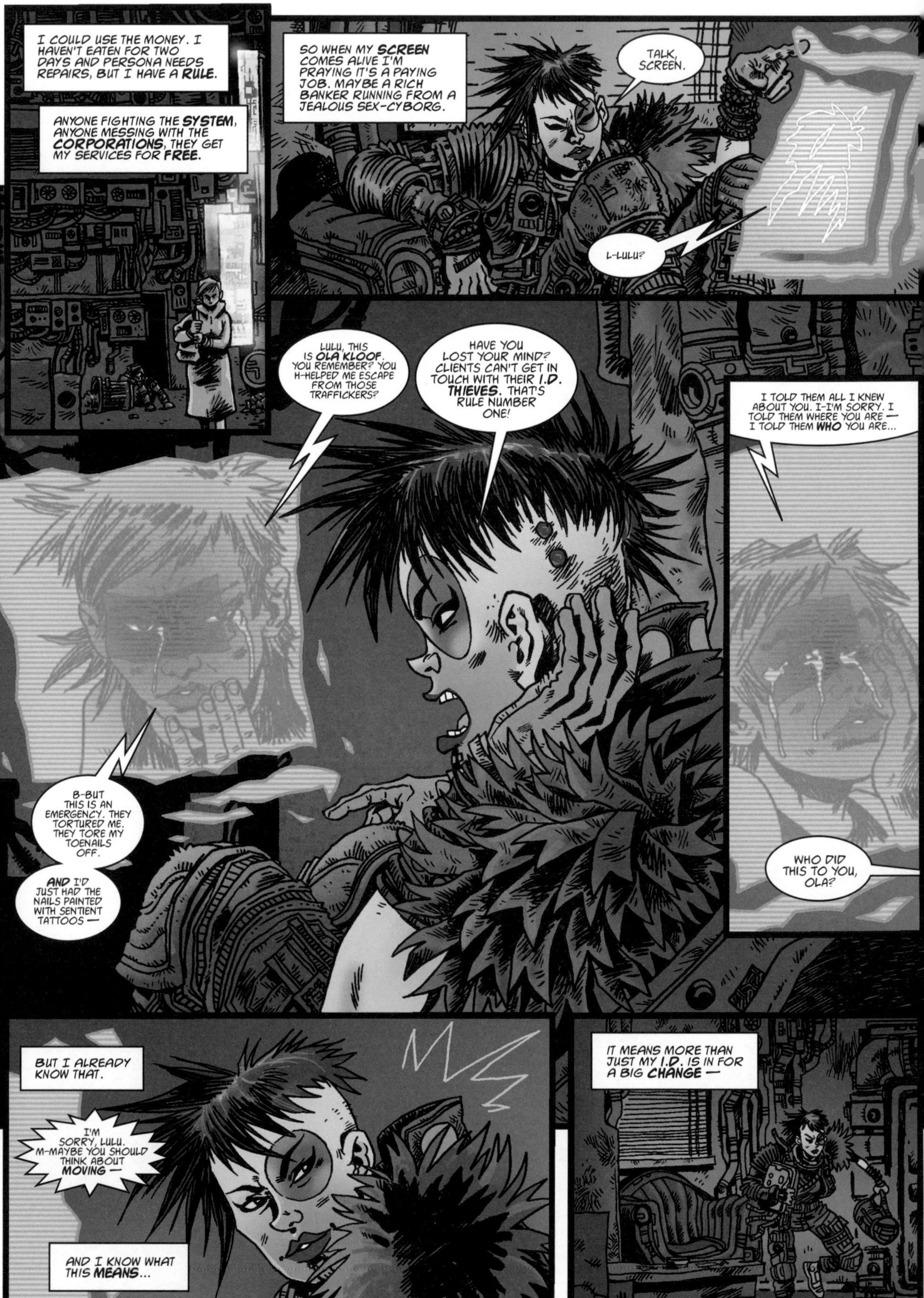

I COULD USE THE MONEY. I HAVEN'T EATEN FOR TWO DAYS AND PERSONA NEEDS REPAIRS, BUT I HAVE A RULE.
ANYONE FIGHTING THE SYSTEM, ANYONE MESSING WITH THE CORPORATIONS, THEY GET MY SERVICES FOR FREE.
SO WHEN MY SCREEN COMES ALIVE I'M PRAYING IT'S A PAYING JOB. MAYBE A RICH BANKER RUNNING FROM A JEALOUS SEX-CYBORG.
TALK, SCREEN.
L-LULU?
LULU, THIS IS OLA KLOOF. YOU REMEMBER? YOU H-HELPED ME ESCAPE FROM THOSE TRAFFICKERS?
HAVE YOU LOST YOUR MIND? CLIENTS CAN'T GET IN TOUCH WITH THEIR I.D. THIEVES. THAT'S RULE NUMBER ONE!
B-BUT THIS IS AN EMERGENCY. THEY TORTURED ME. THEY TORE MY TOENAILS OFF.
AND I'D JUST HAD THE NAILS PAINTED WITH SENTIENT TATTOOS —
I TOLD THEM ALL I KNEW ABOUT YOU. I-I'M SORRY. I TOLD THEM WHERE YOU ARE — I TOLD THEM WHO YOU ARE...
WHO DID THIS TO YOU, OLA?
BUT I ALREADY KNOW THAT.
I'M SORRY, LULU. M-MAYBE YOU SHOULD THINK ABOUT MOVING —
AND I KNOW WHAT THIS MEANS...
IT MEANS MORE THAN JUST MY I.D. IS IN FOR A BIG CHANGE —

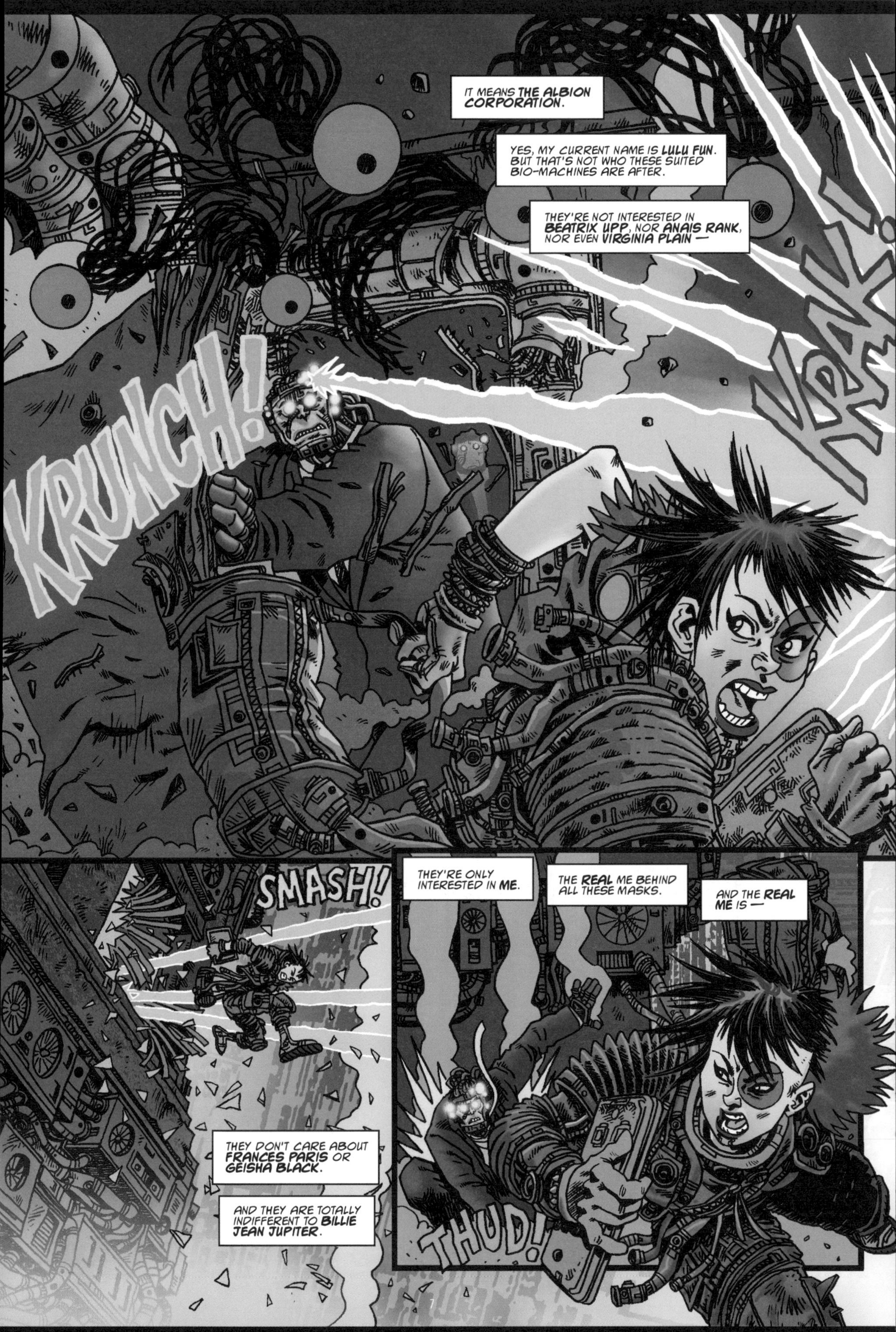
IT MEANS THE ALBION CORPORATION.
YES, MY CURRENT NAME IS LULU FUN. BUT THAT'S NOT WHO THESE SUITED BIO-MACHINES ARE AFTER.
THEY'RE NOT INTERESTED IN BEATRIX UPP, NOR ANAIS RANK, NOR EVEN VIRGINIA PLAIN —
KRUNCH!
KRAK!
SMASH!
THEY DON'T CARE ABOUT FRANCES PARIS OR GEISHA BLACK.
AND THEY ARE TOTALLY INDIFFERENT TO BILLIE JEAN JUPITER.
THEY'RE ONLY INTERESTED IN ME.
THE REAL ME BEHIND ALL THESE MASKS.
AND THE REAL ME IS —
THUD!

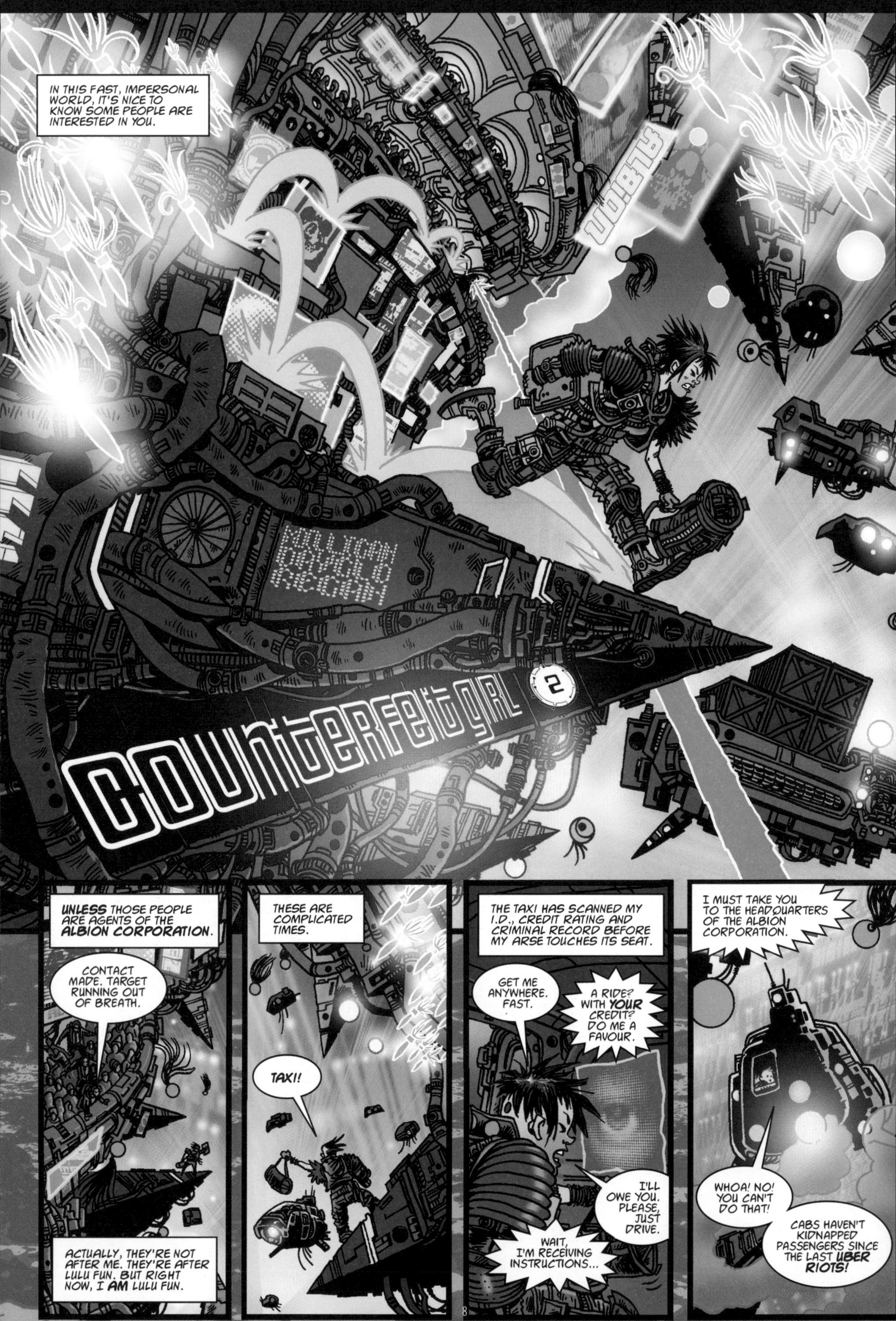
IN THIS FAST, IMPERSONAL WORLD, IT'S NICE TO KNOW SOME PEOPLE ARE INTERESTED IN YOU.
ALBION
COUNTERFEIT GIRL
2
UNLESS THOSE PEOPLE ARE AGENTS OF THE ALBION CORPORATION.
CONTACT MADE. TARGET RUNNING OUT OF BREATH.
ACTUALLY, THEY'RE NOT AFTER ME. THEY'RE AFTER LULU FUN. BUT RIGHT NOW, I AM LULU FUN.
THESE ARE COMPLICATED TIMES.
TAXI!
THE TAXI HAS SCANNED MY I.D., CREDIT RATING AND CRIMINAL RECORD BEFORE MY ARSE TOUCHES ITS SEAT.
GET ME ANYWHERE. FAST.
A RIDE? WITH YOUR CREDIT? DO ME A FAVOUR.
I'LL OWE YOU. PLEASE, JUST DRIVE.
WAIT, I'M RECEIVING INSTRUCTIONS...
I MUST TAKE YOU TO THE HEADQUARTERS OF THE ALBION CORPORATION.
WHOA! NO! YOU CAN'T DO THAT!
CABS HAVEN'T KIDNAPPED PASSENGERS SINCE THE LAST UBER RIOTS!

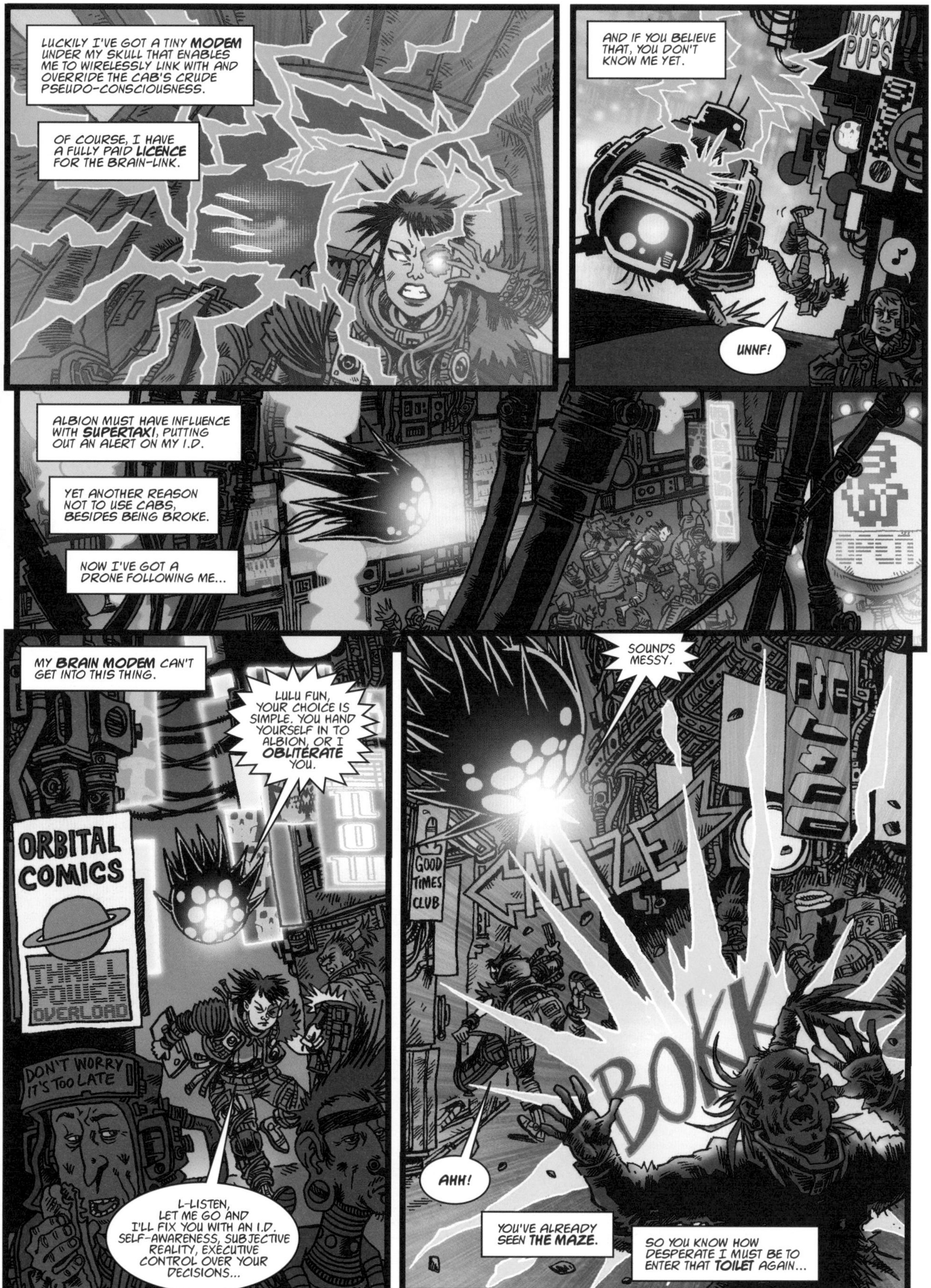
LUCKILY I'VE GOT A TINY MODEM UNDER MY SKULL THAT ENABLES ME TO WIRELESSLY LINK WITH AND OVERRIDE THE CAB'S CRUDE PSEUDO-CONSCIOUSNESS.
OF COURSE, I HAVE A FULLY PAID LICENCE FOR THE BRAIN-LINK.
AND IF YOU BELIEVE THAT, YOU DON'T KNOW ME YET.
MUCKY PUPS
UNNF!
ALBION MUST HAVE INFLUENCE WITH SUPERTAXI, PUTTING OUT AN ALERT ON MY I.D.
YET ANOTHER REASON NOT TO USE CABS, BESIDES BEING BROKE.
NOW I'VE GOT A DRONE FOLLOWING ME...
OPEN
MY BRAIN MODEM CAN'T GET INTO THIS THING.
LULU FUN, YOUR CHOICE IS SIMPLE. YOU HAND YOURSELF IN TO ALBION, OR I OBLITERATE YOU.
ORBITAL COMICS
THRILL POWER OVERLOAD
DON'T WORRY IT'S TOO LATE
L-LISTEN, LET ME GO AND I'LL FIX YOU WITH AN I.D. SELF-AWARENESS, SUBJECTIVE REALITY, EXECUTIVE CONTROL OVER YOUR DECISIONS...
SOUNDS MESSY.
GOOD TIMES CLUB
MAZE
BOKK
AHH!
YOU'VE ALREADY SEEN THE MAZE.
SO YOU KNOW HOW DESPERATE I MUST BE TO ENTER THAT TOILET AGAIN...

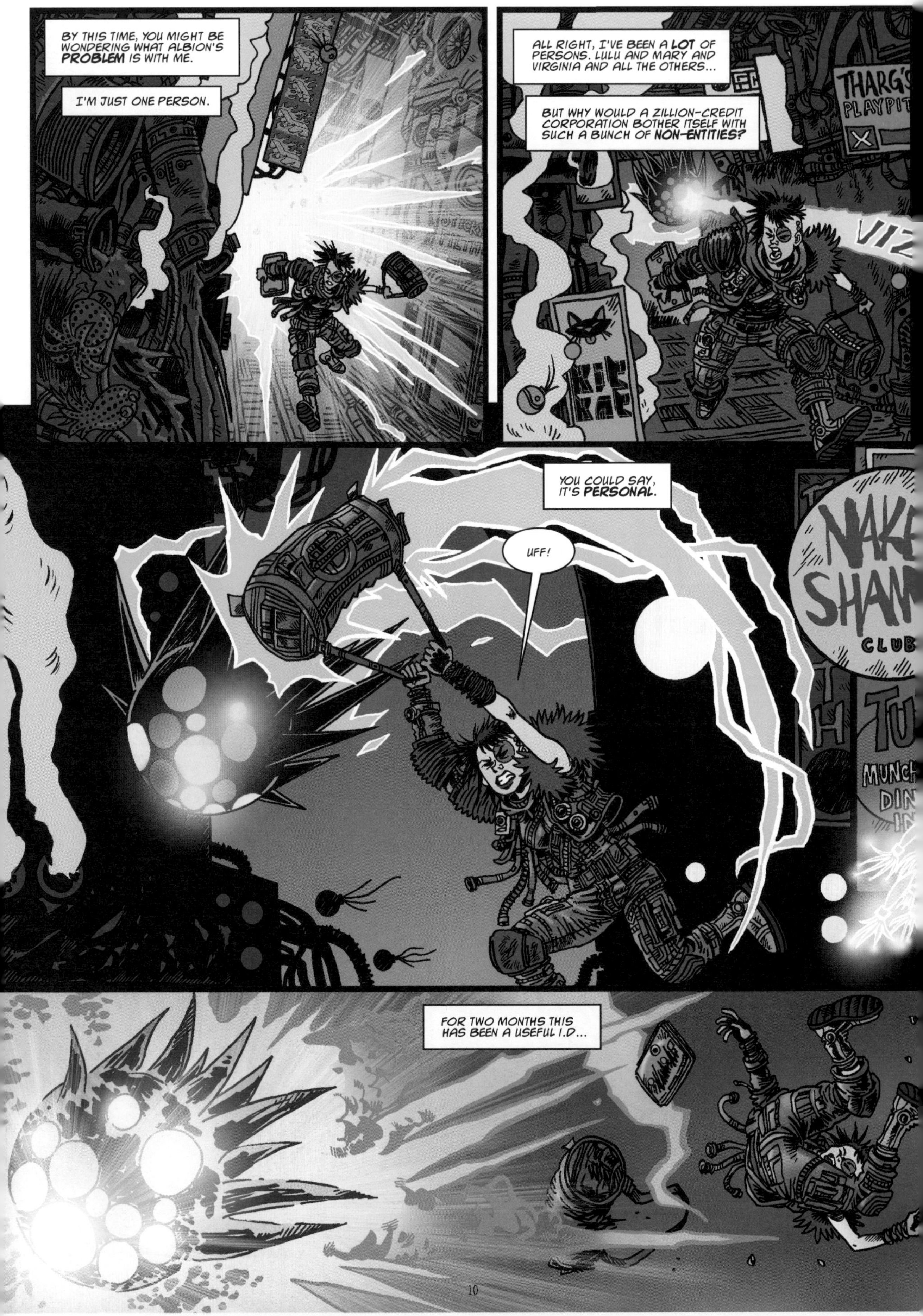
BY THIS TIME, YOU MIGHT BE WONDERING WHAT ALBION'S **PROBLEM** IS WITH ME.
I'M JUST ONE PERSON.
ALL RIGHT, I'VE BEEN A **LOT** OF PERSONS. LULU AND MARY AND VIRGINIA AND ALL THE OTHERS...
BUT WHY WOULD A ZILLION-CREDIT CORPORATION BOTHER ITSELF WITH SUCH A BUNCH OF **NON-ENTITIES?**
THARG'S
KIT KAT
YOU COULD SAY, IT'S **PERSONAL**.
UFF!
CLUB
FOR TWO MONTHS THIS HAS BEEN A USEFUL I.D...

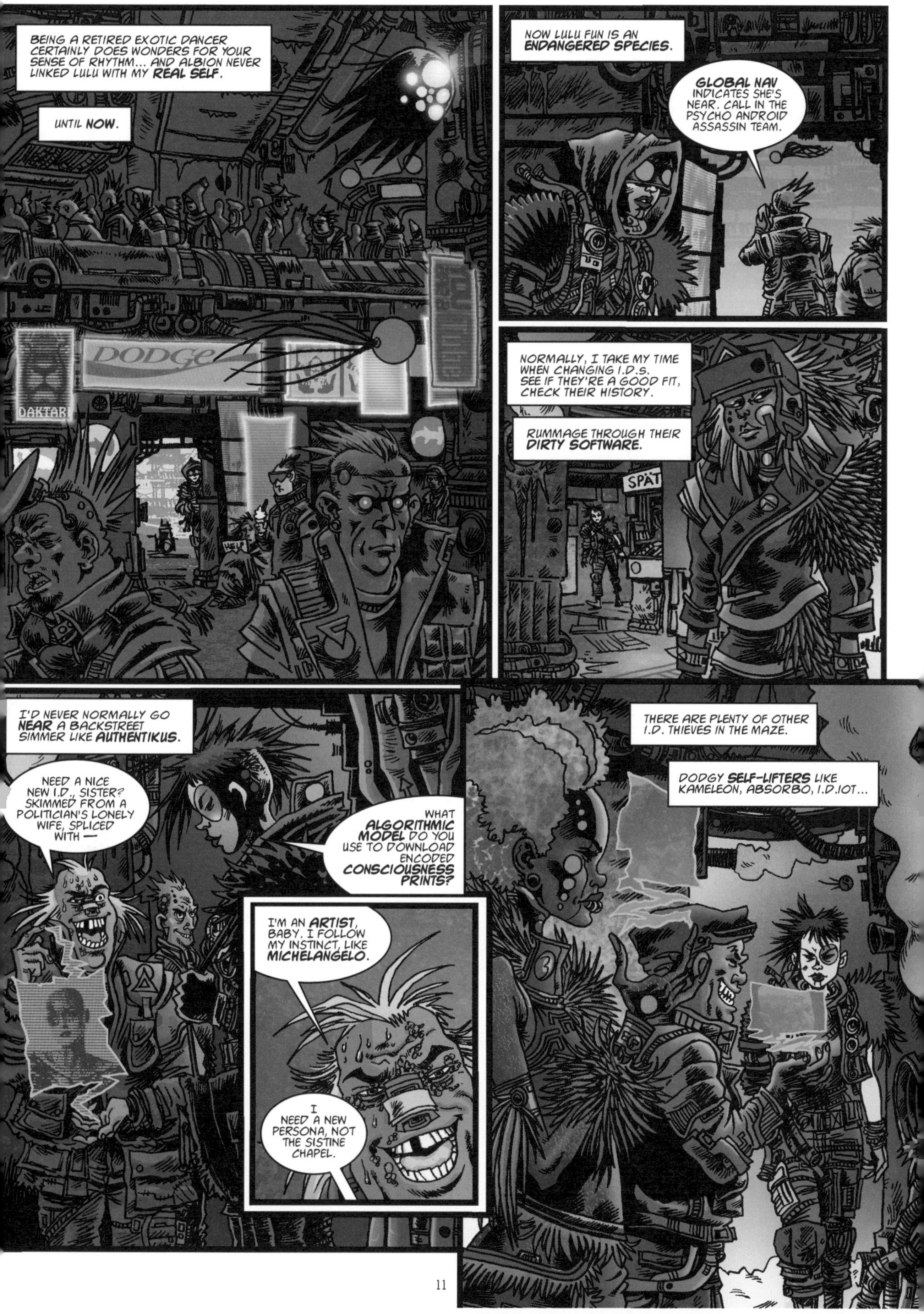
BEING A RETIRED EXOTIC DANCER CERTAINLY DOES WONDERS FOR YOUR SENSE OF RHYTHM... AND ALBION NEVER LINKED LULU WITH MY REAL SELF.
UNTIL NOW.
DODGE
DAKTARI
NOW LULU FUN IS AN ENDANGERED SPECIES.
GLOBAL NAV INDICATES SHE'S NEAR. CALL IN THE PSYCHO ANDROID ASSASSIN TEAM.
NORMALLY, I TAKE MY TIME WHEN CHANGING I.D.s. SEE IF THEY'RE A GOOD FIT, CHECK THEIR HISTORY.
RUMMAGE THROUGH THEIR DIRTY SOFTWARE.
SPÄT
I'D NEVER NORMALLY GO NEAR A BACKSTREET SIMMER LIKE AUTHENTIKUS.
NEED A NICE NEW I.D., SISTER? SKIMMED FROM A POLITICIAN'S LONELY WIFE, SPLICED WITH —
WHAT ALGORITHMIC MODEL DO YOU USE TO DOWNLOAD ENCODED CONSCIOUSNESS PRINTS?
I'M AN ARTIST, BABY. I FOLLOW MY INSTINCT, LIKE MICHELANGELO.
I NEED A NEW PERSONA, NOT THE SISTINE CHAPEL.
THERE ARE PLENTY OF OTHER I.D. THIEVES IN THE MAZE.
DODGY SELF-LIFTERS LIKE KAMELEON, ABSORBO, I.D.IOT...

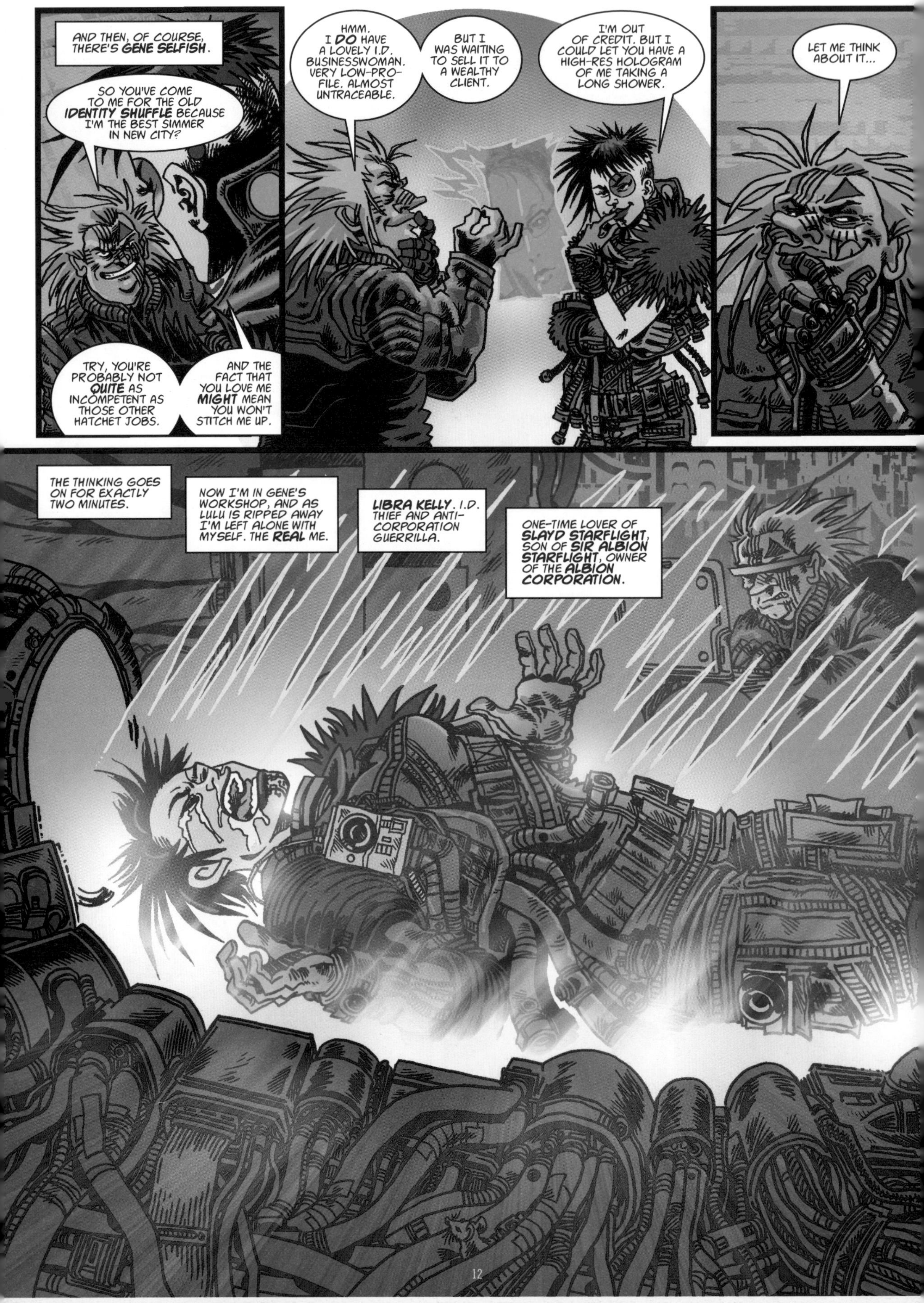
AND THEN, OF COURSE, THERE'S GENE SELFISH.
SO YOU'VE COME TO ME FOR THE OLD IDENTITY SHUFFLE BECAUSE I'M THE BEST SIMMER IN NEW CITY?
TRY, YOU'RE PROBABLY NOT QUITE AS INCOMPETENT AS THOSE OTHER HATCHET JOBS.
AND THE FACT THAT YOU LOVE ME MIGHT MEAN YOU WON'T STITCH ME UP.
HMM. I DO HAVE A LOVELY I.D. BUSINESSWOMAN. VERY LOW-PRO-FILE. ALMOST UNTRACEABLE.
BUT I WAS WAITING TO SELL IT TO A WEALTHY CLIENT.
I'M OUT OF CREDIT. BUT I COULD LET YOU HAVE A HIGH-RES HOLOGRAM OF ME TAKING A LONG SHOWER.
LET ME THINK ABOUT IT...
THE THINKING GOES ON FOR EXACTLY TWO MINUTES.
NOW I'M IN GENE'S WORKSHOP, AND AS LULU IS RIPPED AWAY I'M LEFT ALONE WITH MYSELF. THE REAL ME.
LIBRA KELLY. I.D. THIEF AND ANTI-CORPORATION GUERRILLA.
ONE-TIME LOVER OF SLAYD STARFLIGHT, SON OF SIR ALBION STARFLIGHT, OWNER OF THE ALBION CORPORATION.

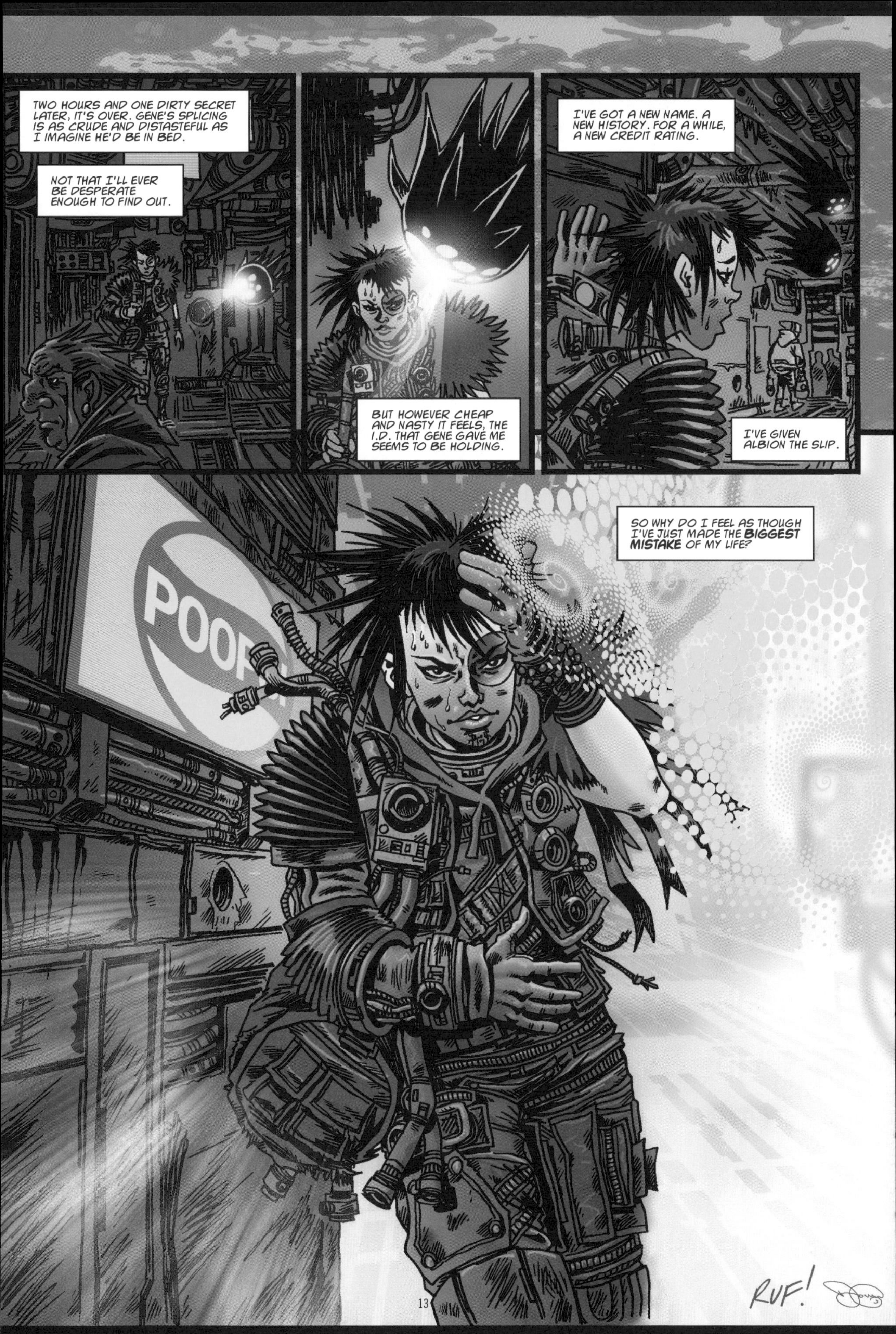

TWO HOURS AND ONE DIRTY SECRET LATER, IT'S OVER. GENE'S SPLICING IS AS CRUDE AND DISTASTEFUL AS I IMAGINE HE'D BE IN BED.
NOT THAT I'LL EVER BE DESPERATE ENOUGH TO FIND OUT.
BUT HOWEVER CHEAP AND NASTY IT FEELS, THE I.D. THAT GENE GAVE ME SEEMS TO BE HOLDING.
I'VE GOT A NEW NAME. A NEW HISTORY. FOR A WHILE, A NEW CREDIT RATING.
I'VE GIVEN ALBION THE SLIP.
POOP
SO WHY DO I FEEL AS THOUGH I'VE JUST MADE THE **BIGGEST MISTAKE** OF MY LIFE?
RUF!

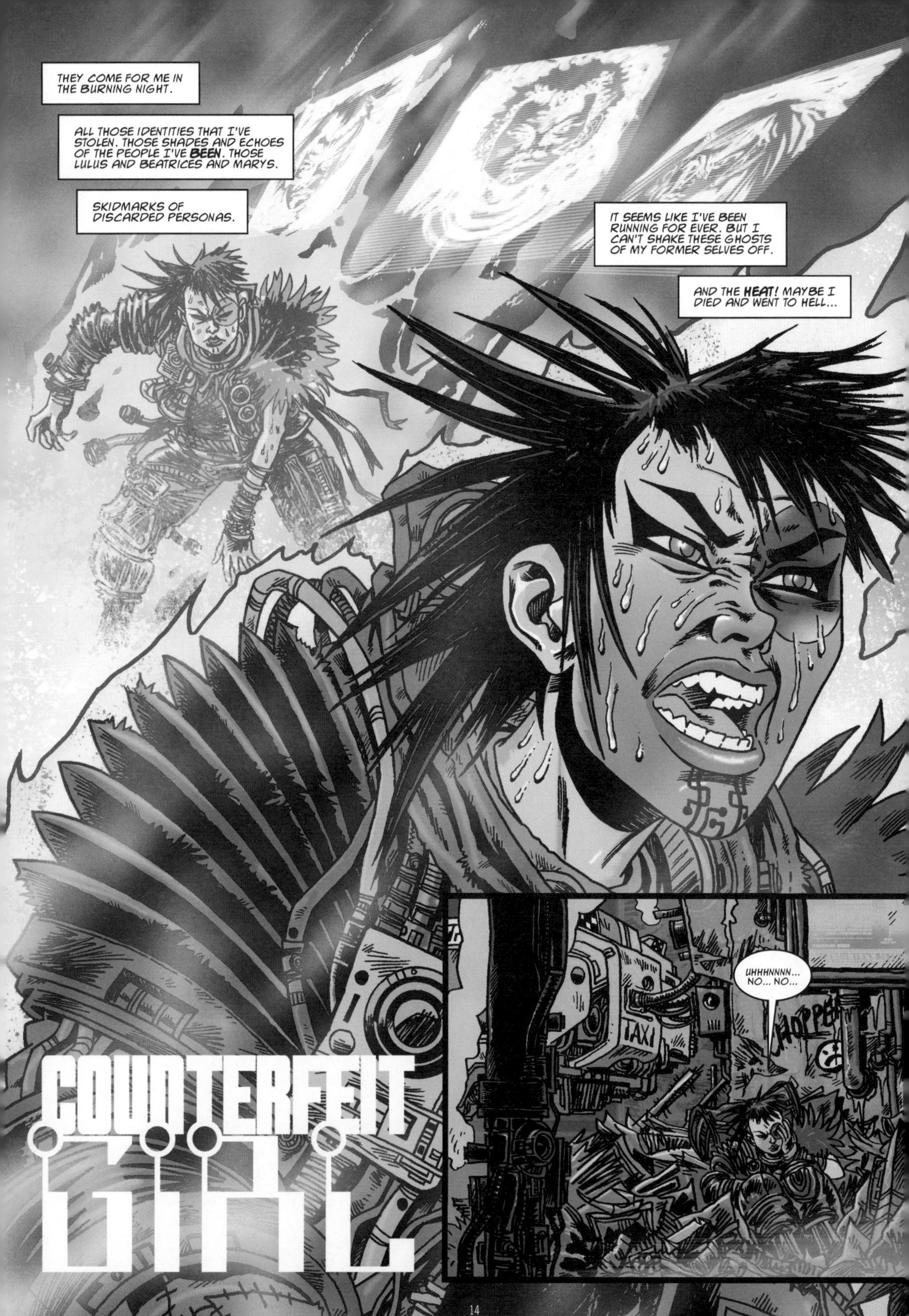
THEY COME FOR ME IN THE BURNING NIGHT.
ALL THOSE IDENTITIES THAT I'VE STOLEN. THOSE SHADES AND ECHOES OF THE PEOPLE I'VE **BEEN**. THOSE LULUS AND BEATRICES AND MARYS.
SKIDMARKS OF DISCARDED PERSONAS.
IT SEEMS LIKE I'VE BEEN RUNNING FOR EVER. BUT I CAN'T SHAKE THESE GHOSTS OF MY FORMER SELVES OFF.
AND THE **HEAT!** MAYBE I DIED AND WENT TO HELL...
COUNTERFEIT GIRL
UHHHNNNN... NO... NO...
TAXI

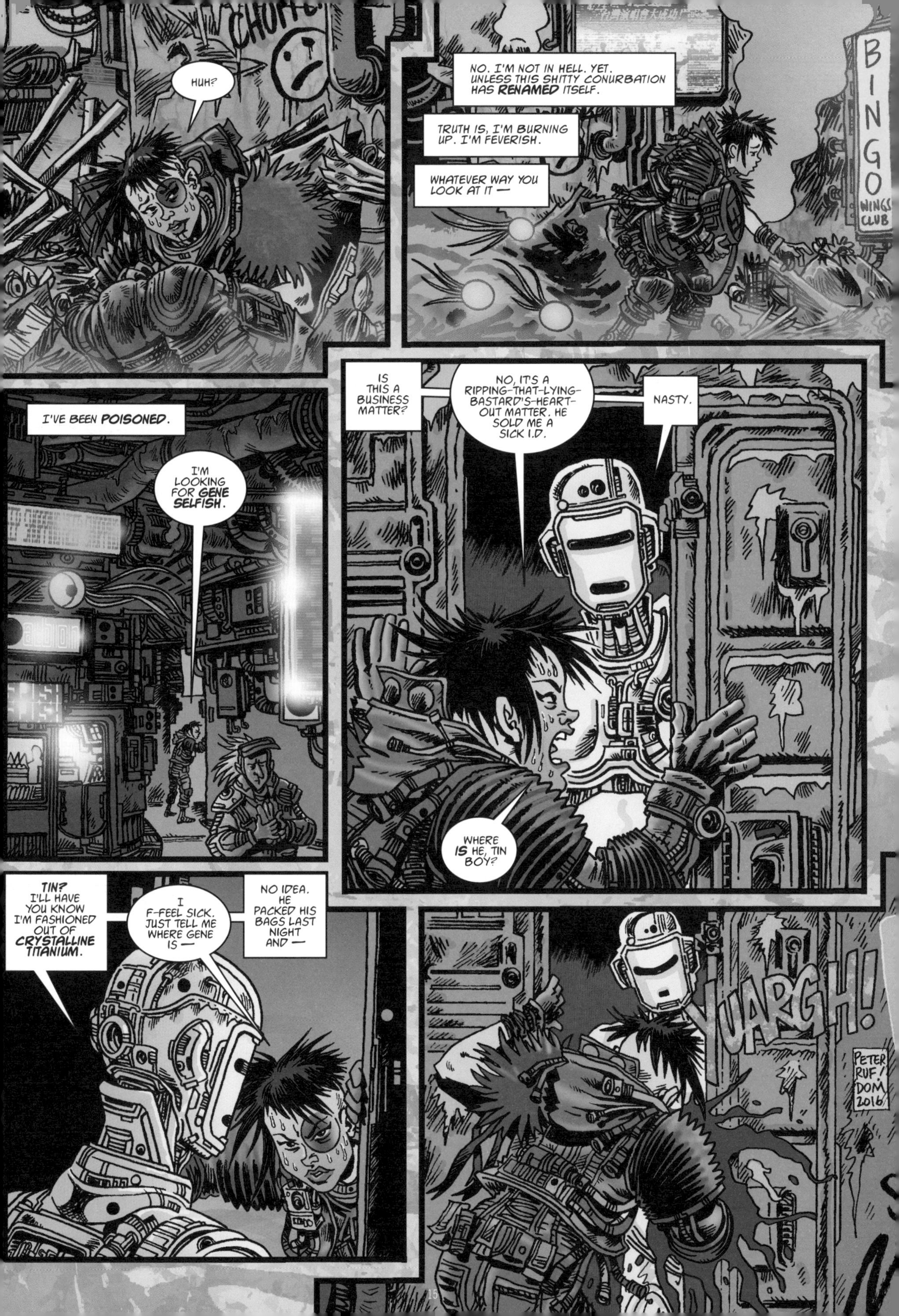
CHUFF
HUH?
NO. I'M NOT IN HELL. YET. UNLESS THIS SHITTY CONURBATION HAS **RENAMED** ITSELF.
TRUTH IS, I'M BURNING UP. I'M FEVERISH.
WHATEVER WAY YOU LOOK AT IT —
BINGO
WINGS CLUB
I'VE BEEN **POISONED**.
I'M LOOKING FOR **GENE SELFISH**.
IS THIS A BUSINESS MATTER?
NO, IT'S A RIPPING-THAT-LYING-BASTARD'S-HEART-OUT MATTER. HE SOLD ME A SICK I.D.
NASTY.
WHERE **IS** HE, TIN BOY?
TIN? I'LL HAVE YOU KNOW I'M FASHIONED OUT OF **CRYSTALLINE TITANIUM**.
I F-FEEL SICK. JUST TELL ME WHERE GENE IS —
NO IDEA. HE PACKED HIS BAGS LAST NIGHT AND —
YUARGH!
PETER RUF / DOM 2016

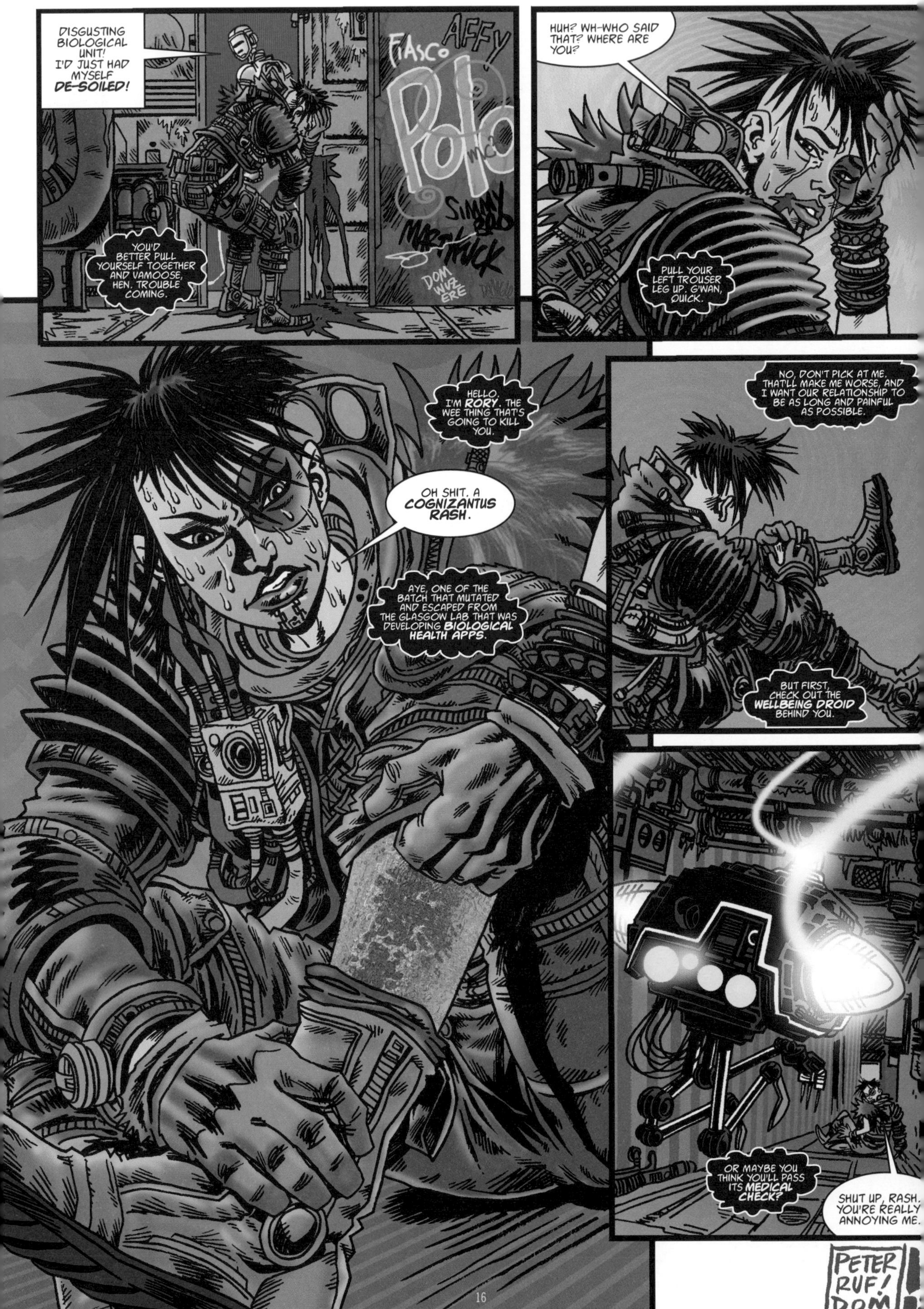
DISGUSTING BIOLOGICAL UNIT! I'D JUST HAD MYSELF DE-SOILED!
FIASCO
AFFY
POLO
SIMMY
MARTY
DOM WUZ ERE
YOU'D BETTER PULL YOURSELF TOGETHER AND VAMOOSE, HEN. TROUBLE COMING.
HUH? WH-WHO SAID THAT? WHERE ARE YOU?
PULL YOUR LEFT TROUSER LEG UP. G'WAN, QUICK.
HELLO, I'M RORY. THE WEE THING THAT'S GOING TO KILL YOU.
OH SHIT. A COGNIZANTUS RASH.
AYE, ONE OF THE BATCH THAT MUTATED AND ESCAPED FROM THE GLASGOW LAB THAT WAS DEVELOPING BIOLOGICAL HEALTH APPS.
NO, DON'T PICK AT ME. THAT'LL MAKE ME WORSE, AND I WANT OUR RELATIONSHIP TO BE AS LONG AND PAINFUL AS POSSIBLE.
BUT FIRST, CHECK OUT THE WELLBEING DROID BEHIND YOU.
OR MAYBE YOU THINK YOU'LL PASS ITS MEDICAL CHECK?
SHUT UP, RASH. YOU'RE REALLY ANNOYING ME.
PETER RUF! DOM

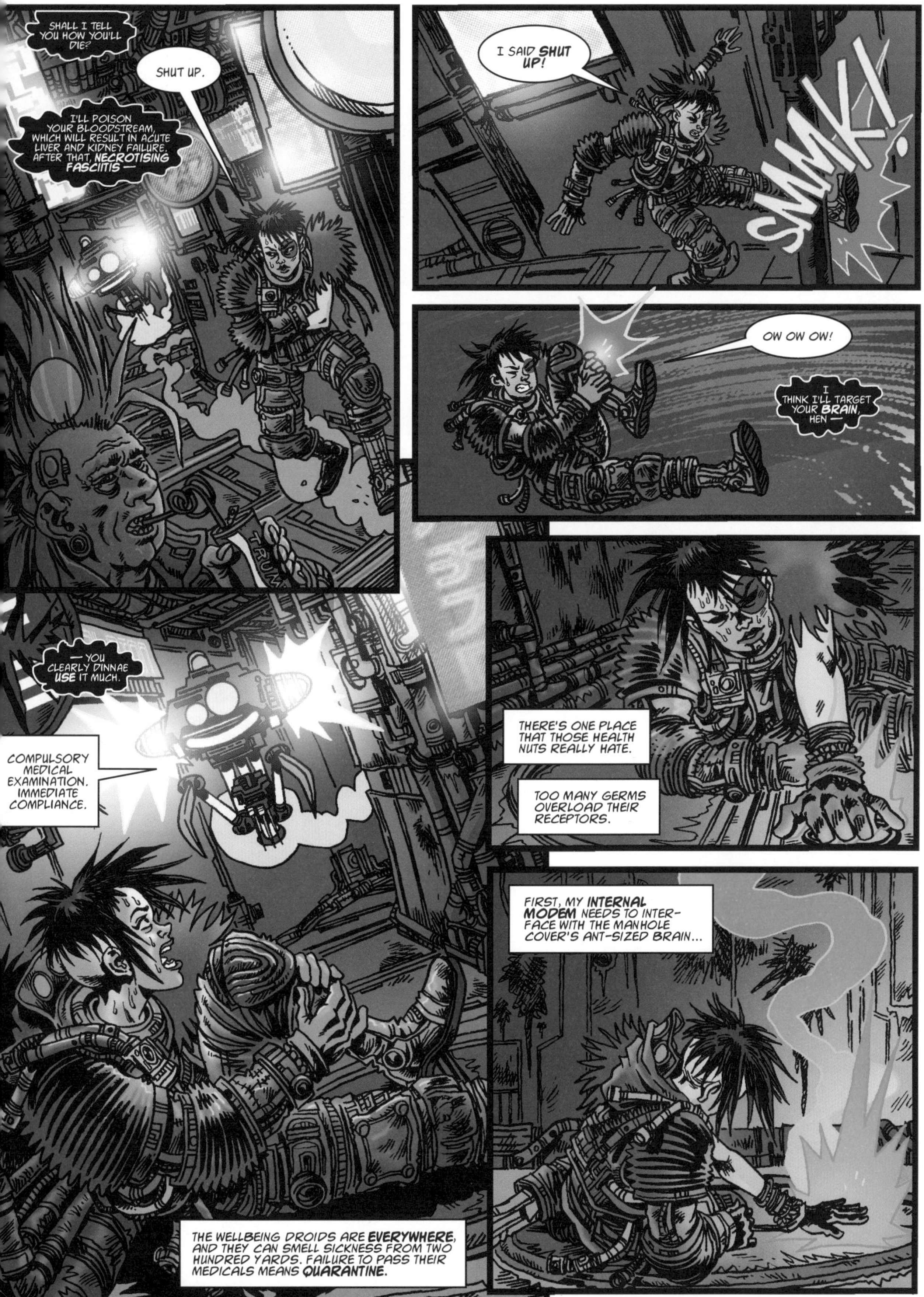
SHALL I TELL YOU HOW YOU'LL DIE?
SHUT UP.
I'LL POISON YOUR BLOODSTREAM, WHICH WILL RESULT IN ACUTE LIVER AND KIDNEY FAILURE. AFTER THAT, NECROTISING FASCIITIS —
I SAID SHUT UP!
SMMK!
OW OW OW!
I THINK I'LL TARGET YOUR BRAIN, HEN —
— YOU CLEARLY DINNAE USE IT MUCH.
COMPULSORY MEDICAL EXAMINATION. IMMEDIATE COMPLIANCE.
THE WELLBEING DROIDS ARE EVERYWHERE, AND THEY CAN SMELL SICKNESS FROM TWO HUNDRED YARDS. FAILURE TO PASS THEIR MEDICALS MEANS QUARANTINE.
THERE'S ONE PLACE THAT THOSE HEALTH NUTS REALLY HATE.
TOO MANY GERMS OVERLOAD THEIR RECEPTORS.
FIRST, MY INTERNAL MODEM NEEDS TO INTER-FACE WITH THE MANHOLE COVER'S ANT-SIZED BRAIN...

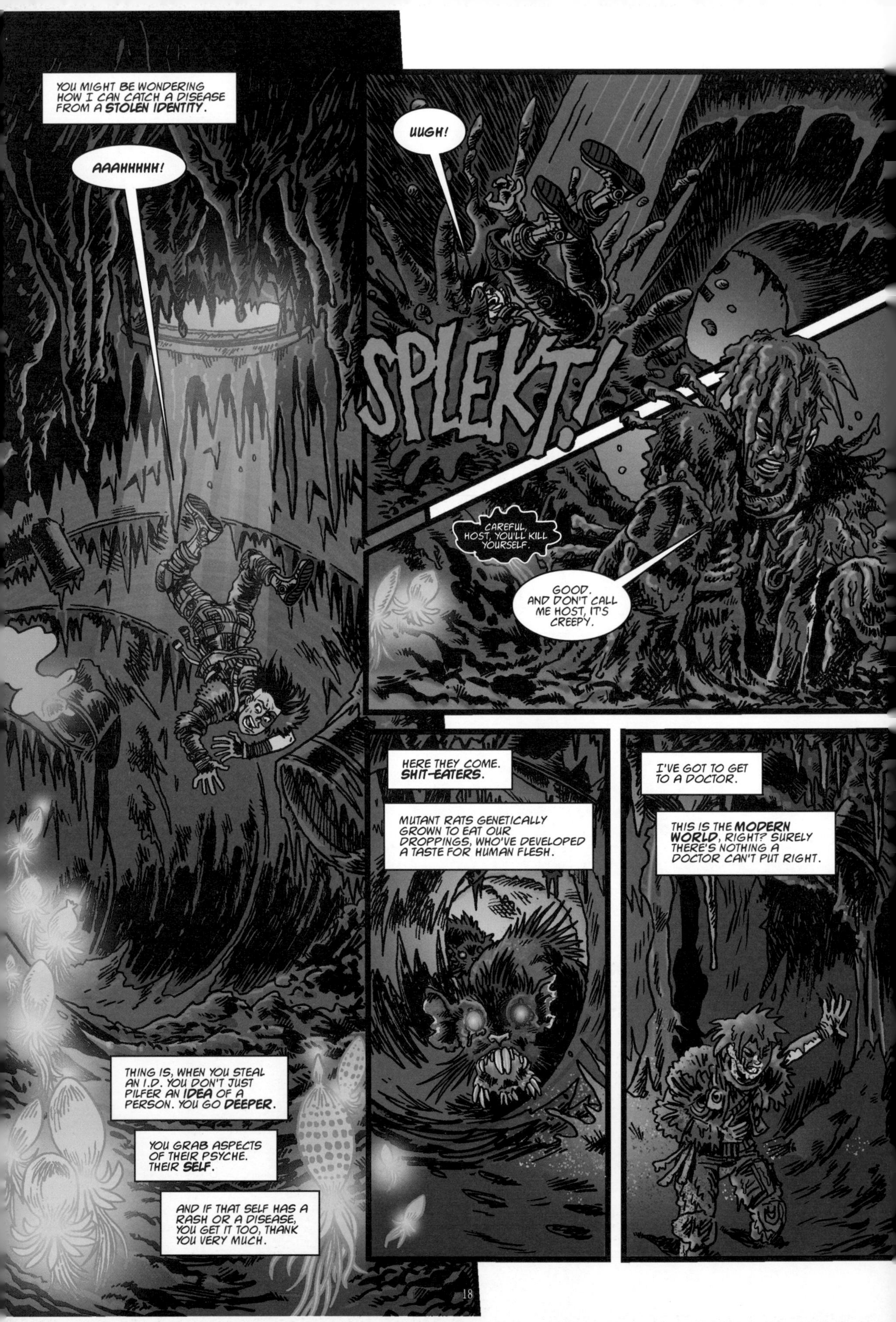
YOU MIGHT BE WONDERING HOW I CAN CATCH A DISEASE FROM A STOLEN IDENTITY.
AAAHHHHH!
THING IS, WHEN YOU STEAL AN I.D. YOU DON'T JUST PILFER AN IDEA OF A PERSON. YOU GO DEEPER.
YOU GRAB ASPECTS OF THEIR PSYCHE. THEIR SELF.
AND IF THAT SELF HAS A RASH OR A DISEASE, YOU GET IT TOO, THANK YOU VERY MUCH.
UUGH!
SPLEKT!
CAREFUL, HOST, YOU'LL KILL YOURSELF.
GOOD. AND DON'T CALL ME HOST, IT'S CREEPY.
HERE THEY COME. SHIT-EATERS.
MUTANT RATS GENETICALLY GROWN TO EAT OUR DROPPINGS, WHO'VE DEVELOPED A TASTE FOR HUMAN FLESH.
I'VE GOT TO GET TO A DOCTOR.
THIS IS THE MODERN WORLD, RIGHT? SURELY THERE'S NOTHING A DOCTOR CAN'T PUT RIGHT.

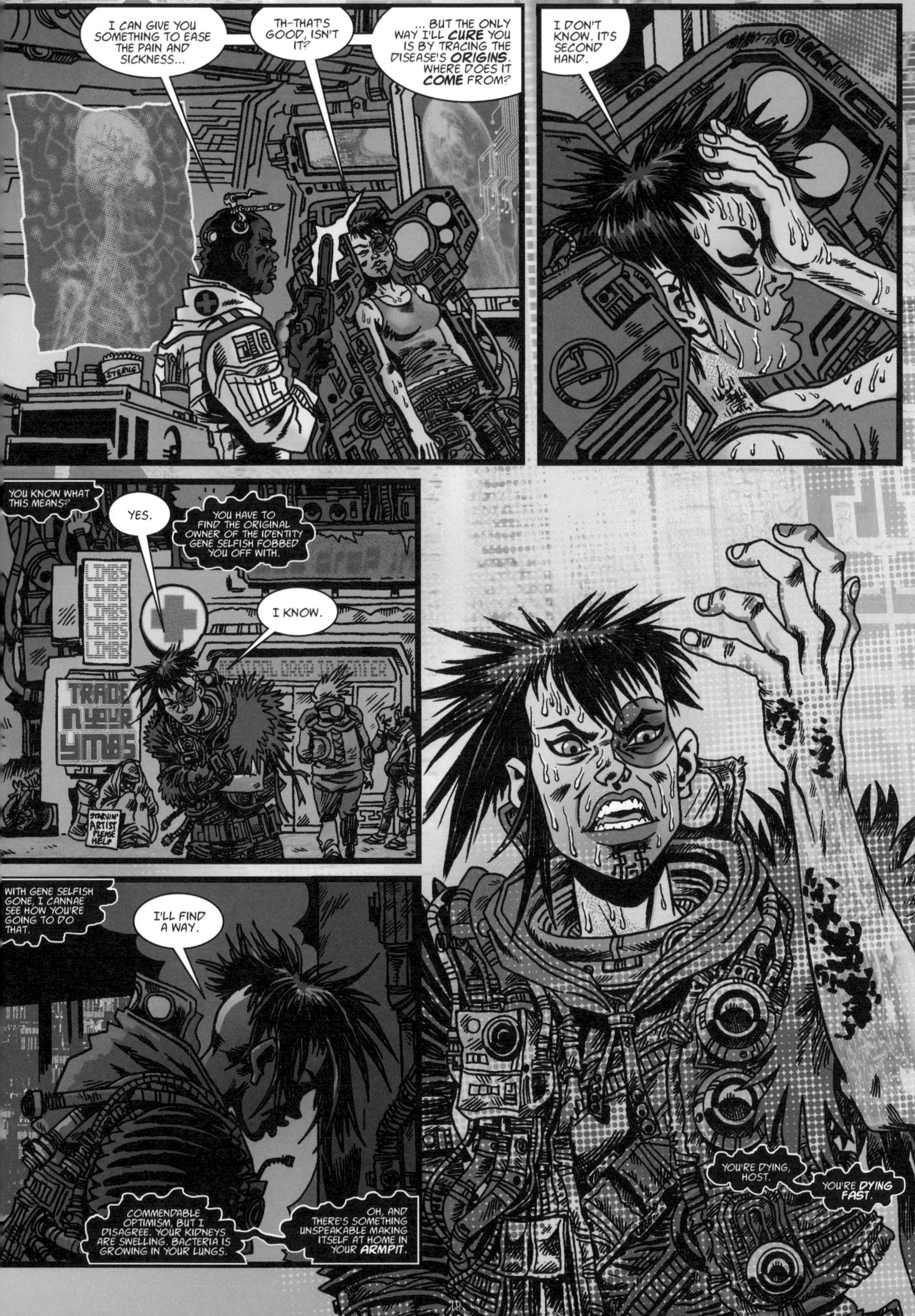

I CAN GIVE YOU SOMETHING TO EASE THE PAIN AND SICKNESS...
TH-THAT'S GOOD, ISN'T IT?
... BUT THE ONLY WAY I'LL **CURE** YOU IS BY TRACING THE DISEASE'S **ORIGINS**. WHERE DOES IT **COME** FROM?
I DON'T KNOW. IT'S SECOND HAND.
YOU KNOW WHAT THIS MEANS?
YES.
YOU HAVE TO FIND THE ORIGINAL OWNER OF THE IDENTITY GENE SELFISH FOBBED YOU OFF WITH.
I KNOW.
STARVIN' ARTIST PLEASE HELP
WITH GENE SELFISH GONE, I CANNAE SEE HOW YOU'RE GOING TO DO THAT.
I'LL FIND A WAY.
COMMENDABLE OPTIMISM, BUT I DISAGREE. YOUR KIDNEYS ARE SWELLING. BACTERIA IS GROWING IN YOUR LUNGS.
OH, AND THERE'S SOMETHING UNSPEAKABLE MAKING ITSELF AT HOME IN YOUR **ARMPIT**.
YOU'RE DYING, HOST.
YOU'RE **DYING FAST**.

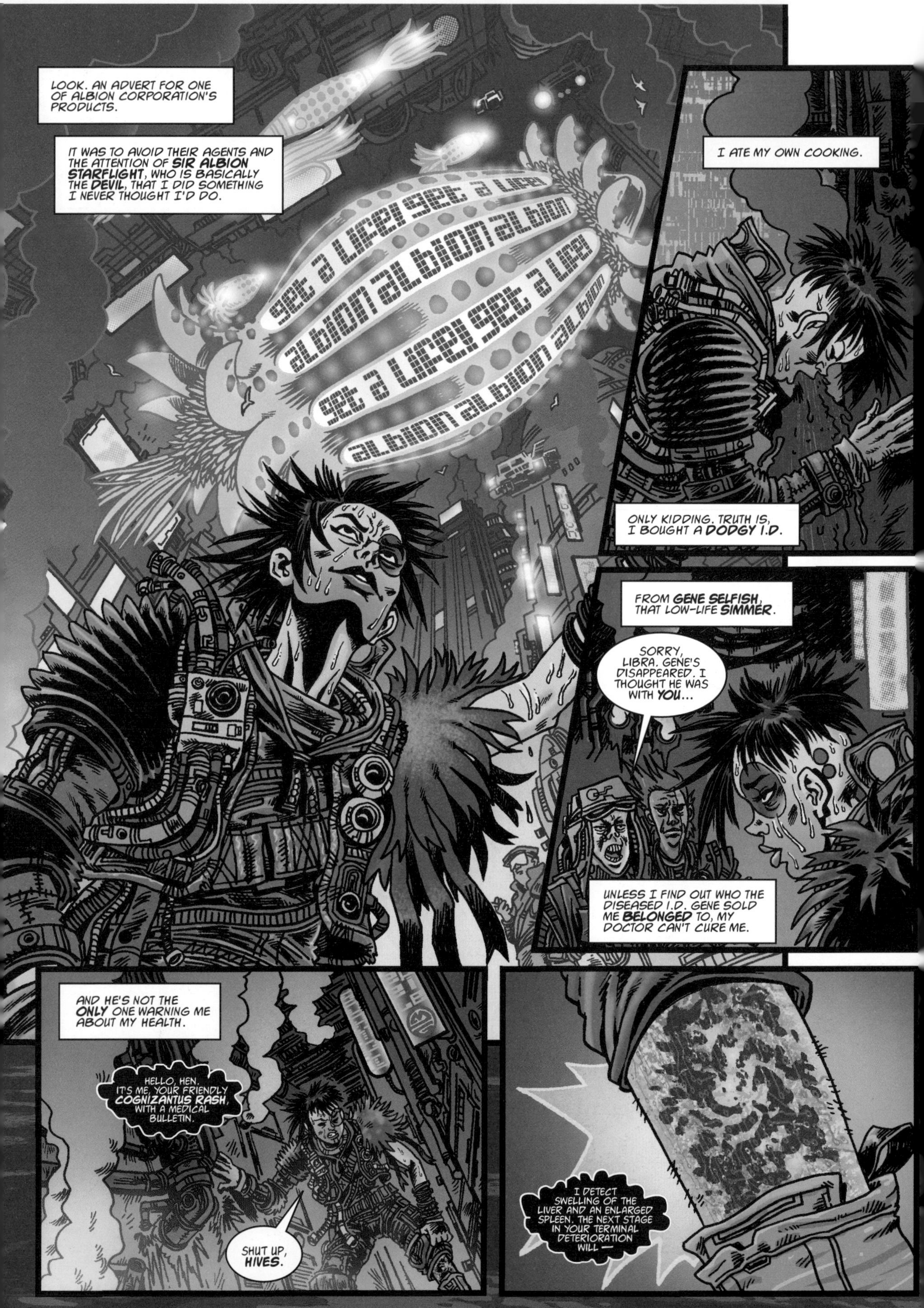

LOOK. AN ADVERT FOR ONE OF ALBION CORPORATION'S PRODUCTS.
IT WAS TO AVOID THEIR AGENTS AND THE ATTENTION OF SIR ALBION STARFLIGHT, WHO IS BASICALLY THE DEVIL, THAT I DID SOMETHING I NEVER THOUGHT I'D DO.
GET A LIFE! GET A LIFE!
ALBION ALBION ALBION
I ATE MY OWN COOKING.
ONLY KIDDING. TRUTH IS, I BOUGHT A DODGY I.D.
FROM GENE SELFISH, THAT LOW-LIFE SIMMER.
SORRY, LIBRA. GENE'S DISAPPEARED. I THOUGHT HE WAS WITH YOU...
UNLESS I FIND OUT WHO THE DISEASED I.D. GENE SOLD ME BELONGED TO, MY DOCTOR CAN'T CURE ME.
AND HE'S NOT THE ONLY ONE WARNING ME ABOUT MY HEALTH.
HELLO, HEN. IT'S ME, YOUR FRIENDLY COGNIZANTUS RASH, WITH A MEDICAL BULLETIN.
SHUT UP, HIVES.
I DETECT SWELLING OF THE LIVER AND AN ENLARGED SPLEEN. THE NEXT STAGE IN YOUR TERMINAL DETERIORATION WILL —

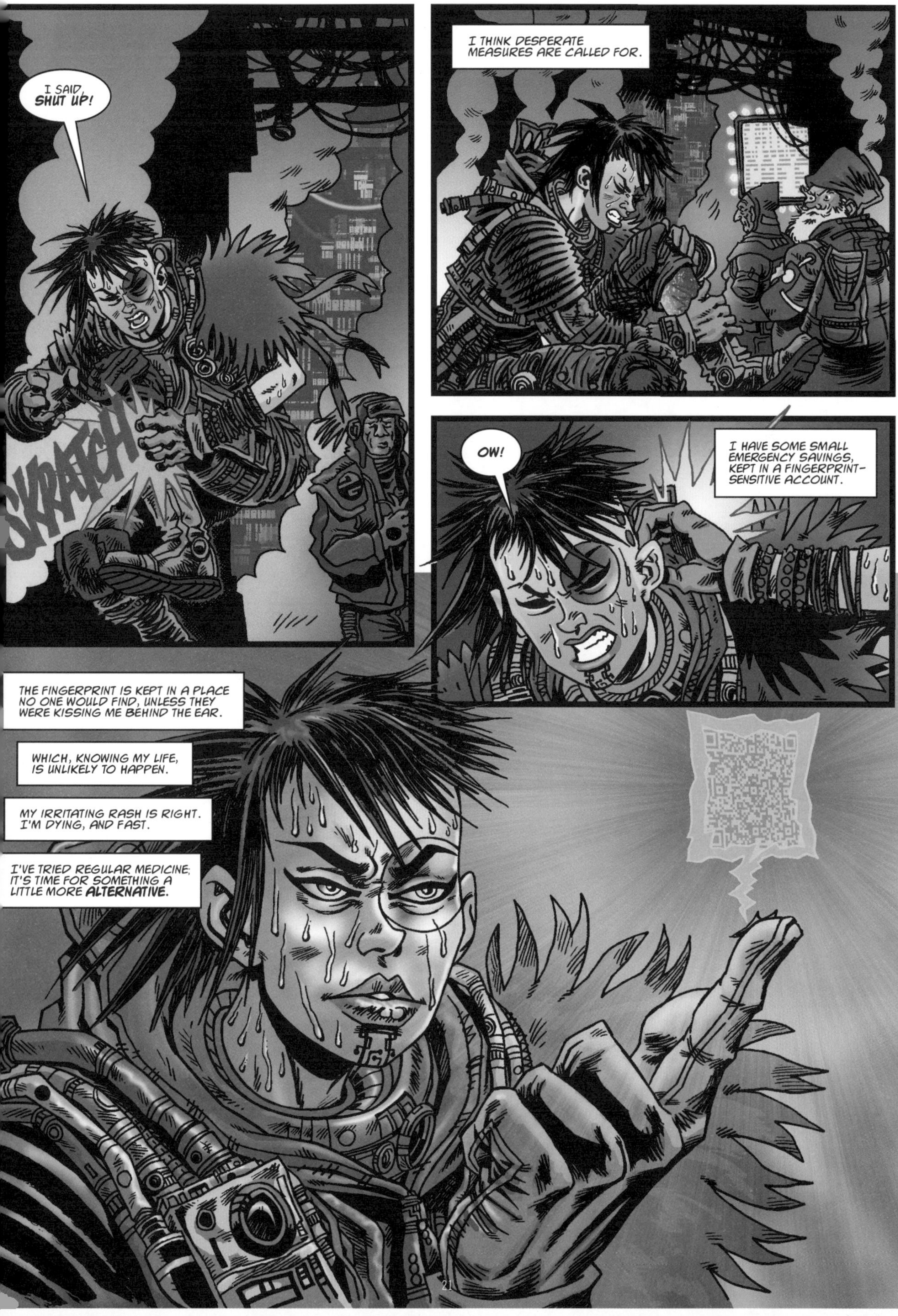
I SAID, SHUT UP!
SKRATCH
I THINK DESPERATE MEASURES ARE CALLED FOR.
OW!
I HAVE SOME SMALL EMERGENCY SAVINGS, KEPT IN A FINGERPRINT-SENSITIVE ACCOUNT.
THE FINGERPRINT IS KEPT IN A PLACE NO ONE WOULD FIND, UNLESS THEY WERE KISSING ME BEHIND THE EAR.
WHICH, KNOWING MY LIFE, IS UNLIKELY TO HAPPEN.
MY IRRITATING RASH IS RIGHT. I'M DYING, AND FAST.
I'VE TRIED REGULAR MEDICINE; IT'S TIME FOR SOMETHING A LITTLE MORE ALTERNATIVE.

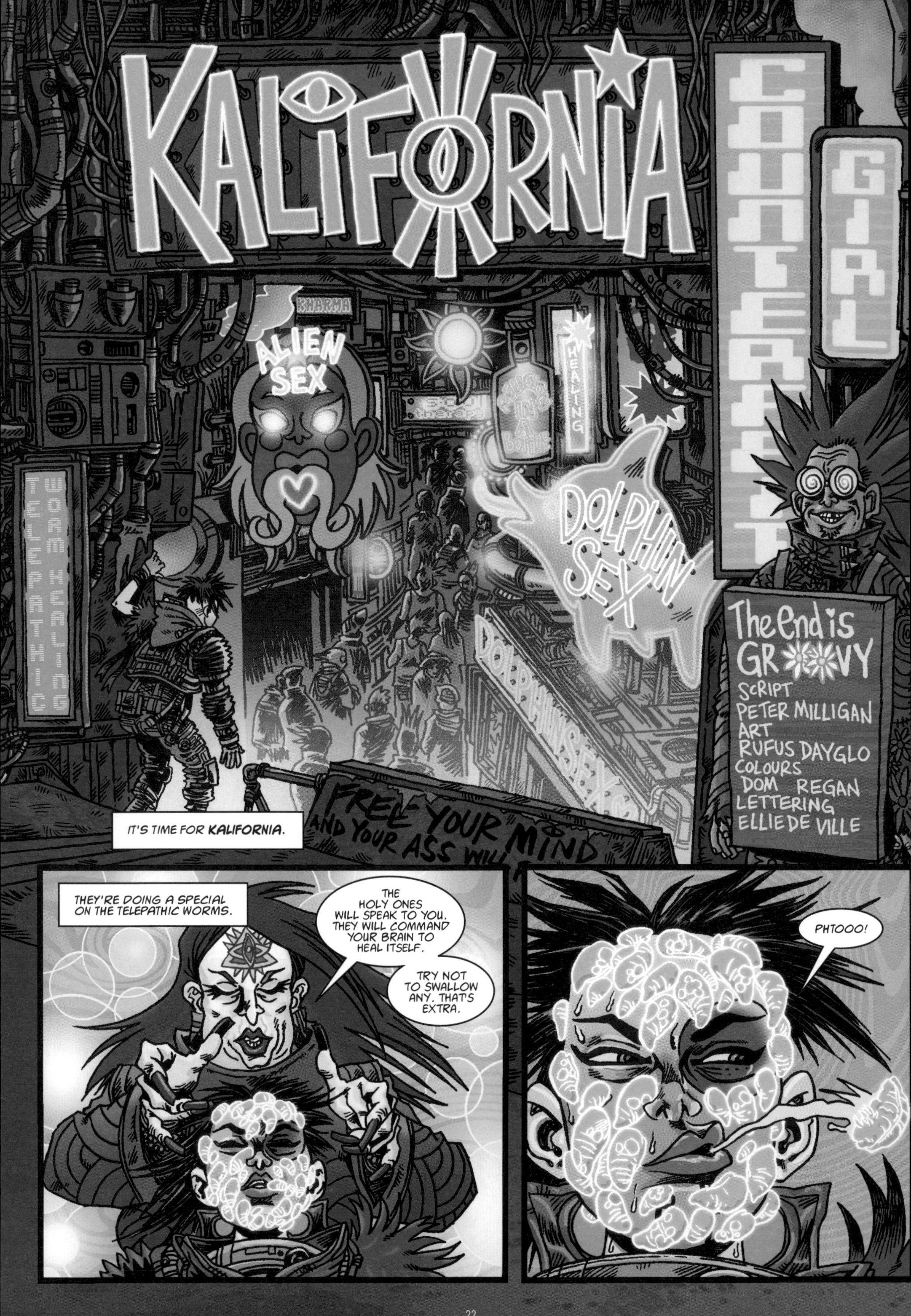
KALIFORNIA
COUNTERFEIT
GIRL
KHARMA
ALIEN SEX
SOUL therapy
HEALING
TELEPATHIC WORM HEALING
DOLPHIN SEX
DOLPHIN SEX
The end is GROOVY
SCRIPT PETER MILLIGAN
ART RUFUS DAYGLO
COLOURS DOM REGAN
LETTERING ELLIE DE VILLE
IT'S TIME FOR **KALIFORNIA**.
FREE YOUR MIND AND YOUR ASS WILL
THEY'RE DOING A SPECIAL ON THE TELEPATHIC WORMS.
THE HOLY ONES WILL SPEAK TO YOU. THEY WILL COMMAND YOUR BRAIN TO HEAL ITSELF.
TRY NOT TO SWALLOW ANY. THAT'S EXTRA.
PHTOOO!

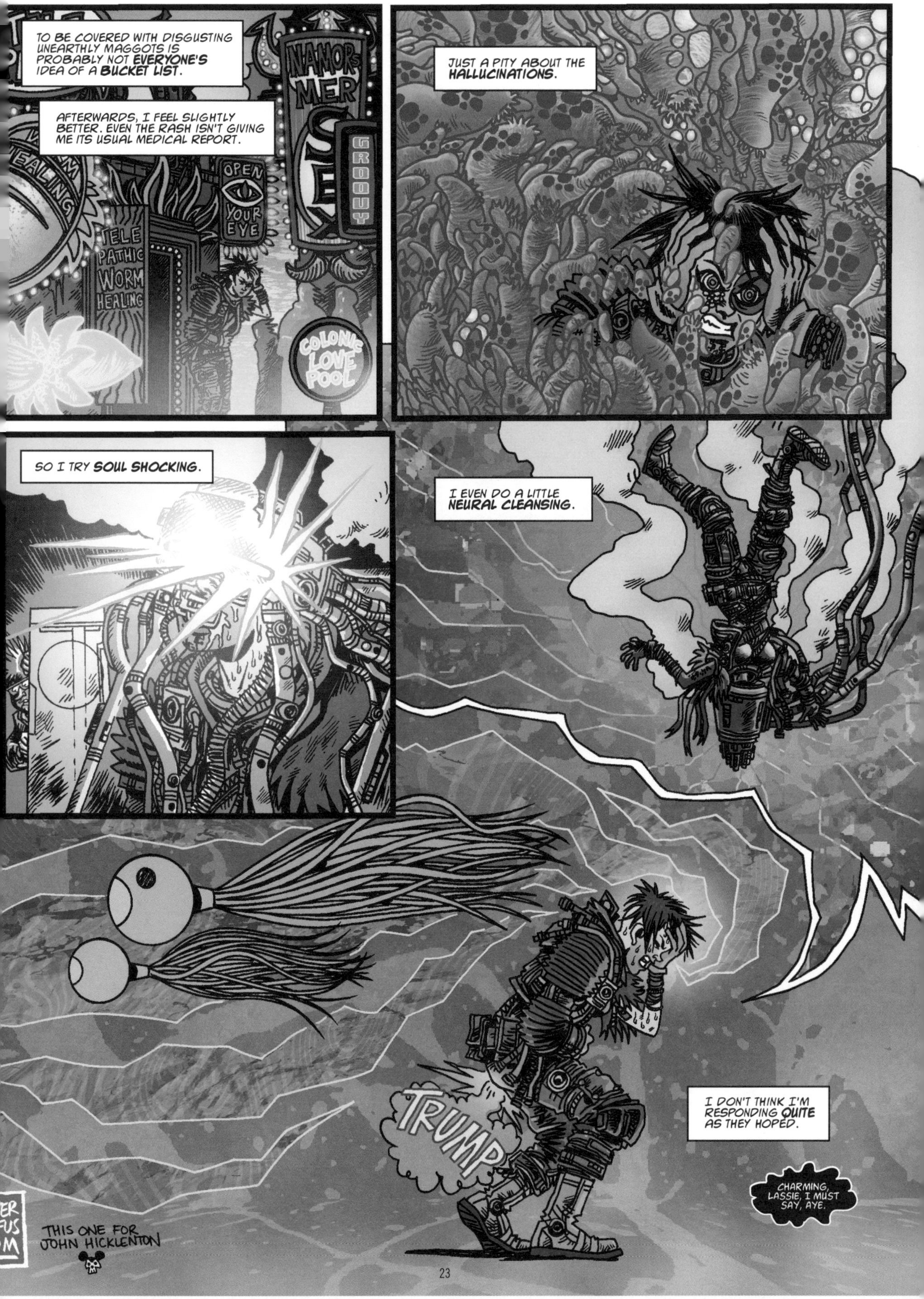

TO BE COVERED WITH DISGUSTING UNEARTHLY MAGGOTS IS PROBABLY NOT **EVERYONE'S** IDEA OF A **BUCKET LIST**.
AFTERWARDS, I FEEL SLIGHTLY BETTER. EVEN THE RASH ISN'T GIVING ME ITS USUAL MEDICAL REPORT.
OPEN YOUR EYE
TELE PATHIC WORM HEALING
GROOVY
COLONIC LOVE POOL
JUST A PITY ABOUT THE **HALLUCINATIONS**.
SO I TRY **SOUL SHOCKING**.
I EVEN DO A LITTLE **NEURAL CLEANSING**.
TRUMP
I DON'T THINK I'M RESPONDING **QUITE** AS THEY HOPED.
CHARMING, LASSIE, I MUST SAY, AYE.
THIS ONE FOR JOHN HICKLENTON

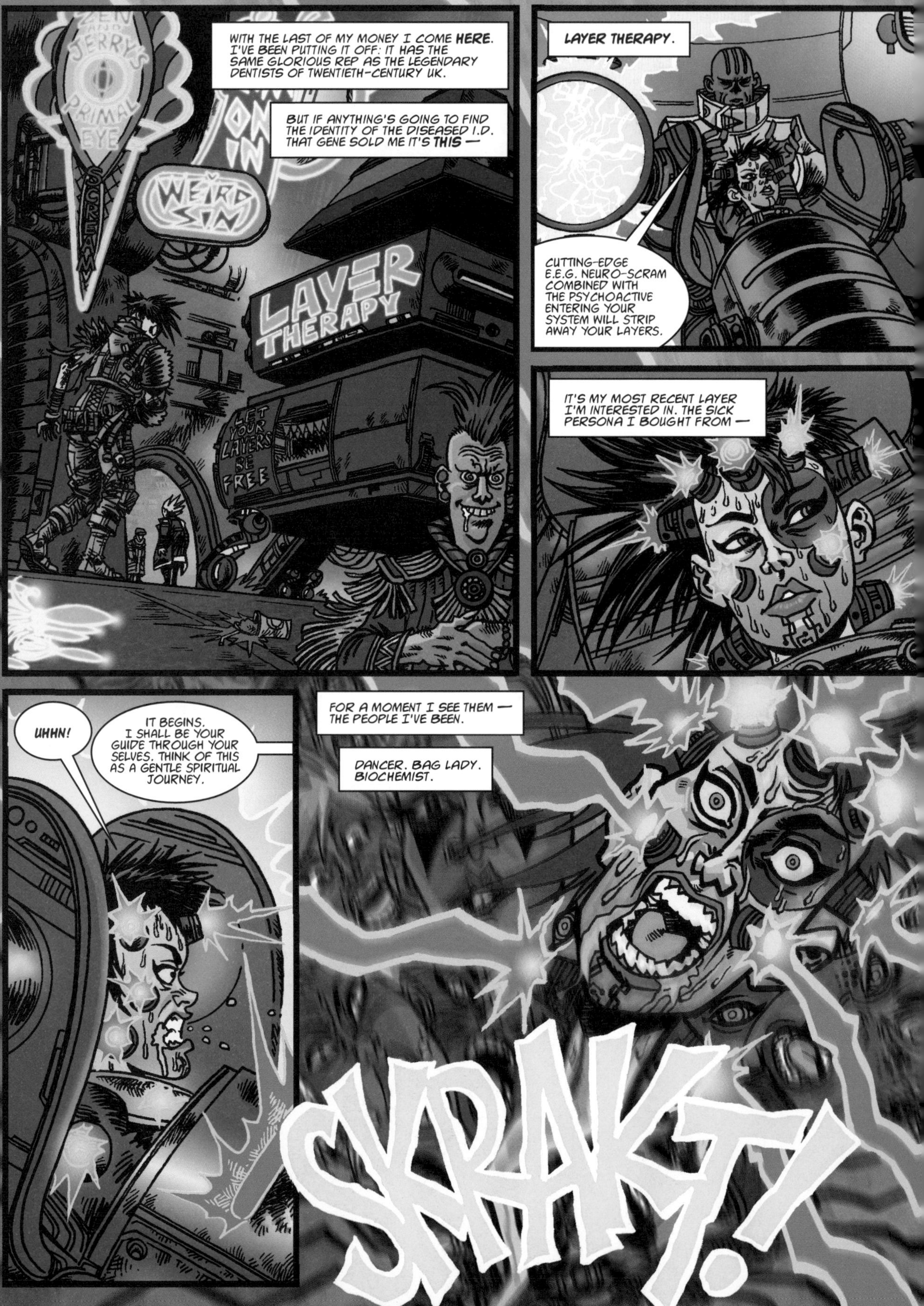

WITH THE LAST OF MY MONEY I COME HERE. I'VE BEEN PUTTING IT OFF: IT HAS THE SAME GLORIOUS REP AS THE LEGENDARY DENTISTS OF TWENTIETH-CENTURY UK.
BUT IF ANYTHING'S GOING TO FIND THE IDENTITY OF THE DISEASED I.D. THAT GENE SOLD ME IT'S THIS —
ZEN AND JERRY'S PRIMAL EYE SCREAM
WEIRD SIN
LAYER THERAPY
LET YOUR LAYERS BE FREE
LAYER THERAPY.
CUTTING-EDGE E.E.G. NEURO-SCRAM COMBINED WITH THE PSYCHOACTIVE ENTERING YOUR SYSTEM WILL STRIP AWAY YOUR LAYERS.
IT'S MY MOST RECENT LAYER I'M INTERESTED IN. THE SICK PERSONA I BOUGHT FROM —
UHHN!
IT BEGINS. I SHALL BE YOUR GUIDE THROUGH YOUR SELVES. THINK OF THIS AS A GENTLE SPIRITUAL JOURNEY.
FOR A MOMENT I SEE THEM — THE PEOPLE I'VE BEEN.
DANCER. BAG LADY. BIOCHEMIST.
SKRAKT!

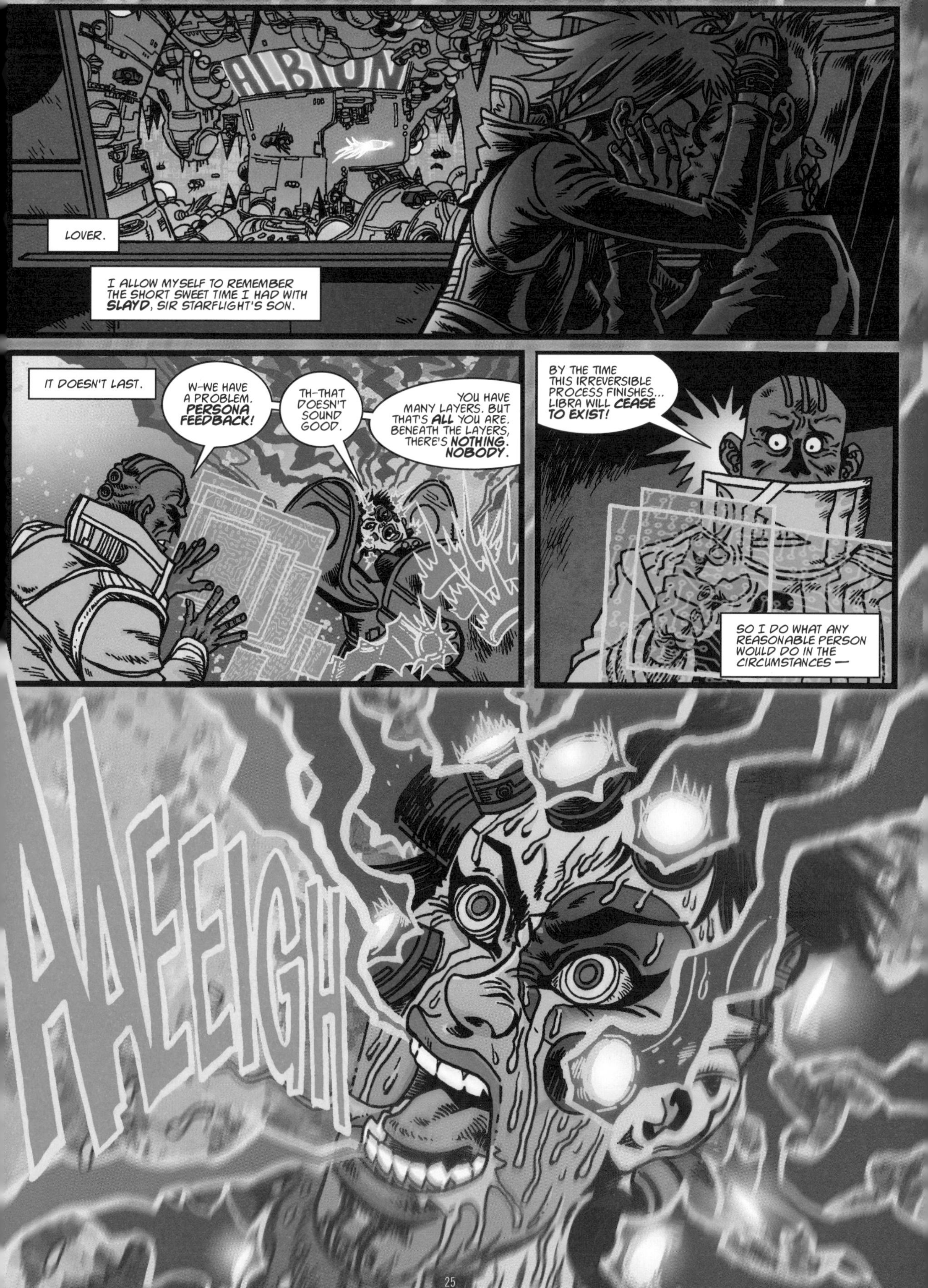
ALBION
LOVER.
I ALLOW MYSELF TO REMEMBER THE SHORT SWEET TIME I HAD WITH SLAYD, SIR STARFLIGHT'S SON.
IT DOESN'T LAST.
W-WE HAVE A PROBLEM. PERSONA FEEDBACK!
TH-THAT DOESN'T SOUND GOOD.
YOU HAVE MANY LAYERS. BUT THAT'S ALL YOU ARE. BENEATH THE LAYERS, THERE'S NOTHING. NOBODY.
BY THE TIME THIS IRREVERSIBLE PROCESS FINISHES... LIBRA WILL CEASE TO EXIST!
SO I DO WHAT ANY REASONABLE PERSON WOULD DO IN THE CIRCUMSTANCES —
AAEEIGH

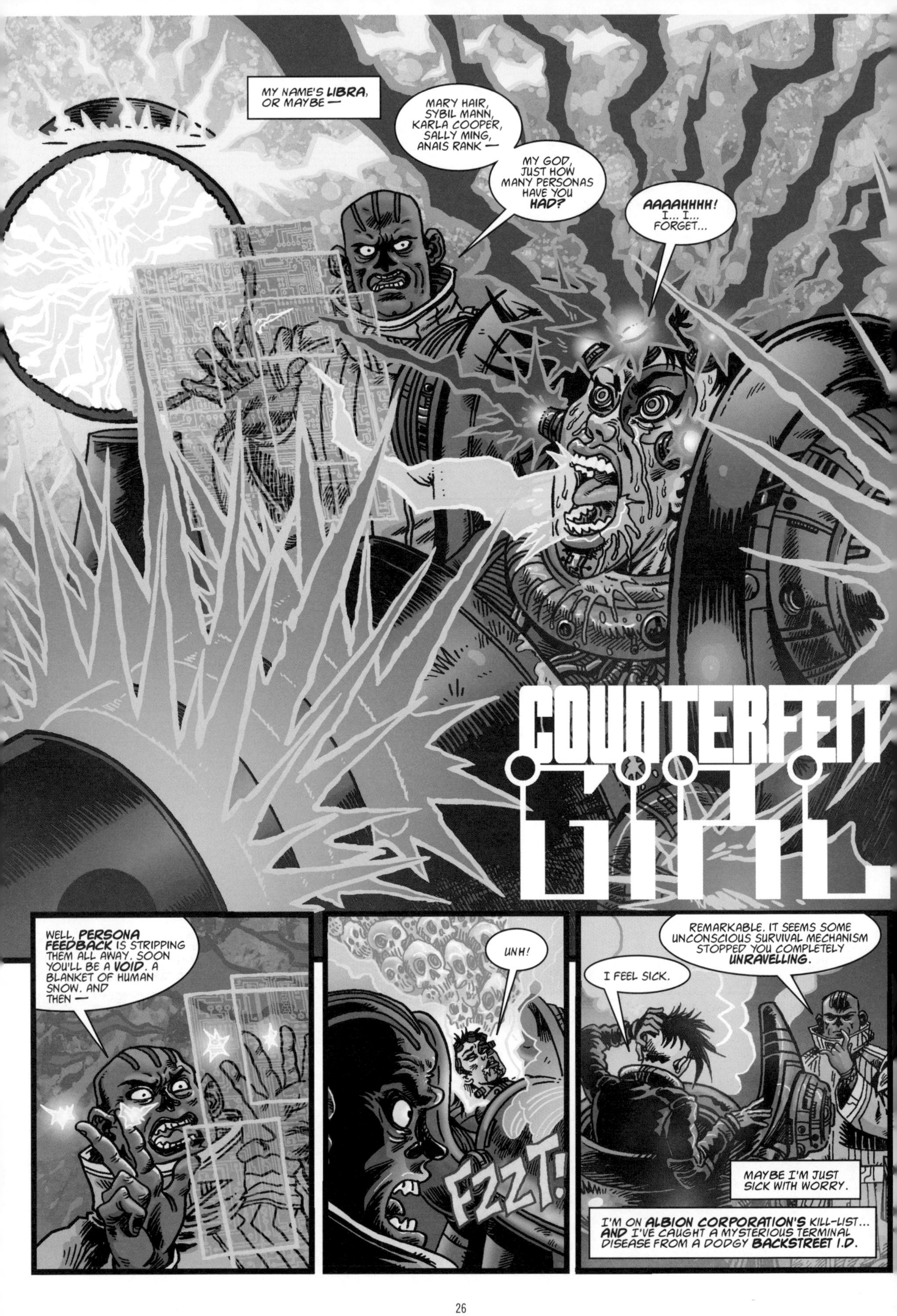

MY NAME'S LIBRA, OR MAYBE —
MARY HAIR, SYBIL MANN, KARLA COOPER, SALLY MING, ANAIS RANK —
MY GOD, JUST HOW MANY PERSONAS HAVE YOU HAD?
AAAAHHHH! I... I... FORGET...
COUNTERFEIT GIRL
WELL, PERSONA FEEDBACK IS STRIPPING THEM ALL AWAY. SOON YOU'LL BE A VOID. A BLANKET OF HUMAN SNOW. AND THEN —
UNH!
FZZT!
REMARKABLE. IT SEEMS SOME UNCONSCIOUS SURVIVAL MECHANISM STOPPED YOU COMPLETELY UNRAVELLING.
I FEEL SICK.
MAYBE I'M JUST SICK WITH WORRY.
I'M ON ALBION CORPORATION'S KILL-LIST... AND I'VE CAUGHT A MYSTERIOUS TERMINAL DISEASE FROM A DODGY BACKSTREET I.D.

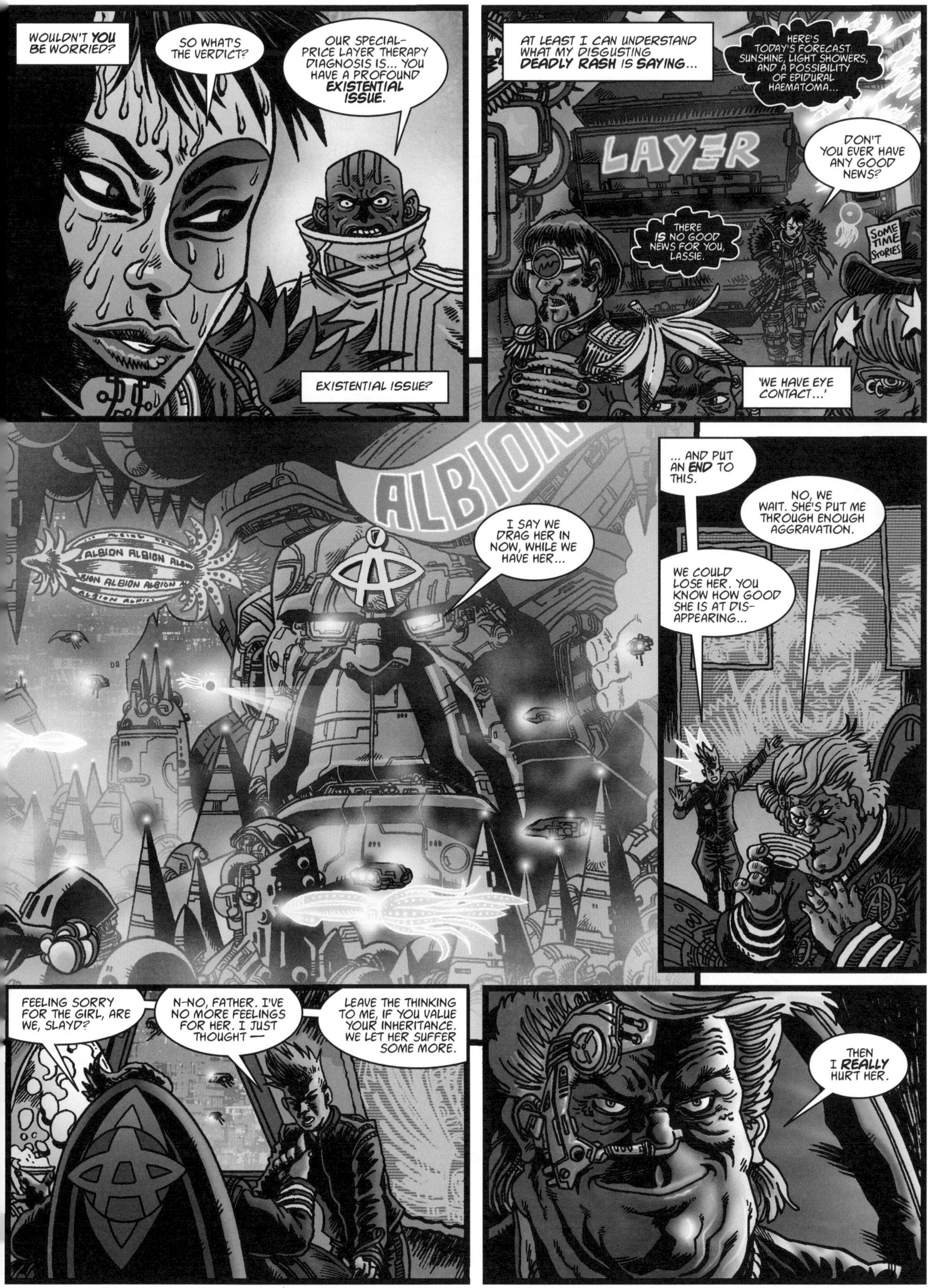
WOULDN'T YOU BE WORRIED?
SO WHAT'S THE VERDICT?
OUR SPECIAL-PRICE LAYER THERAPY DIAGNOSIS IS... YOU HAVE A PROFOUND EXISTENTIAL ISSUE.
EXISTENTIAL ISSUE?
AT LEAST I CAN UNDERSTAND WHAT MY DISGUSTING DEADLY RASH IS SAYING...
HERE'S TODAY'S FORECAST: SUNSHINE, LIGHT SHOWERS, AND A POSSIBILITY OF EPIDURAL HAEMATOMA...
LAYER
DON'T YOU EVER HAVE ANY GOOD NEWS?
THERE IS NO GOOD NEWS FOR YOU, LASSIE.
SOME TIME STORIES
'WE HAVE EYE CONTACT...'
ALBION
I SAY WE DRAG HER IN NOW, WHILE WE HAVE HER...
... AND PUT AN END TO THIS.
NO, WE WAIT. SHE'S PUT ME THROUGH ENOUGH AGGRAVATION.
WE COULD LOSE HER. YOU KNOW HOW GOOD SHE IS AT DIS-APPEARING...
FEELING SORRY FOR THE GIRL, ARE WE, SLAYD?
N-NO, FATHER. I'VE NO MORE FEELINGS FOR HER. I JUST THOUGHT —
LEAVE THE THINKING TO ME, IF YOU VALUE YOUR INHERITANCE. WE LET HER SUFFER SOME MORE.
THEN I REALLY HURT HER.

THIS ONE FOR GARRY LEACH!

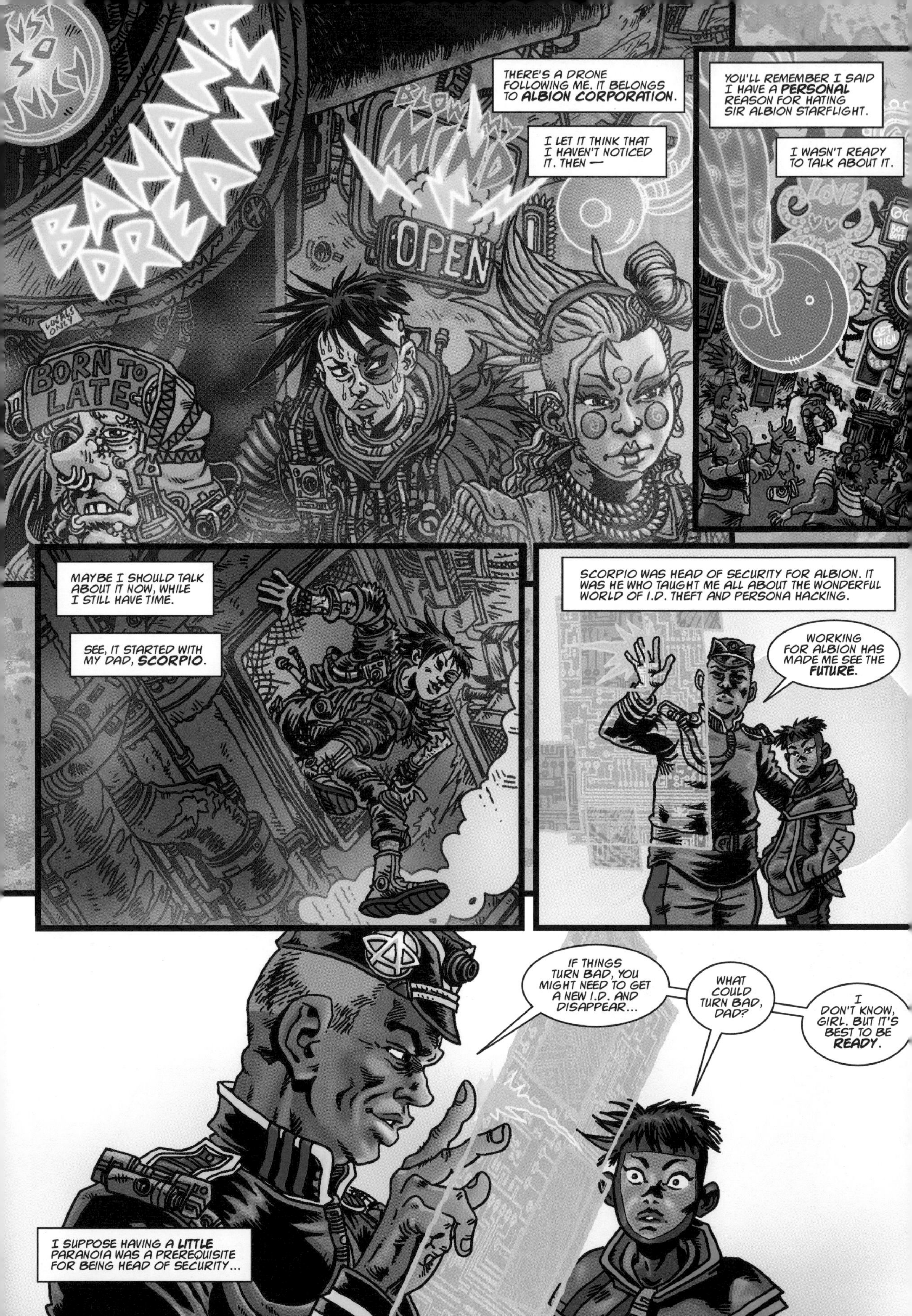
JUST SO JUICY
BANANA DREAMS
THERE'S A DRONE FOLLOWING ME. IT BELONGS TO **ALBION CORPORATION**.
BLOW MY MIND
I LET IT THINK THAT I HAVEN'T NOTICED IT. THEN —
OPEN
LOCALS ONLY
BORN TO LATE
YOU'LL REMEMBER I SAID I HAVE A **PERSONAL** REASON FOR HATING SIR ALBION STARFLIGHT.
I WASN'T READY TO TALK ABOUT IT.
LOVE
GET HIGH
MAYBE I SHOULD TALK ABOUT IT NOW, WHILE I STILL HAVE TIME.
SEE, IT STARTED WITH MY DAD, **SCORPIO**.
SCORPIO WAS HEAD OF SECURITY FOR ALBION. IT WAS HE WHO TAUGHT ME ALL ABOUT THE WONDERFUL WORLD OF I.D. THEFT AND PERSONA HACKING.
WORKING FOR ALBION HAS MADE ME SEE THE **FUTURE**.
IF THINGS TURN BAD, YOU MIGHT NEED TO GET A NEW I.D. AND DISAPPEAR...
WHAT COULD TURN BAD, DAD?
I DON'T KNOW, GIRL. BUT IT'S BEST TO BE **READY**.
I SUPPOSE HAVING A **LITTLE** PARANOIA WAS A PREREQUISITE FOR BEING HEAD OF SECURITY...

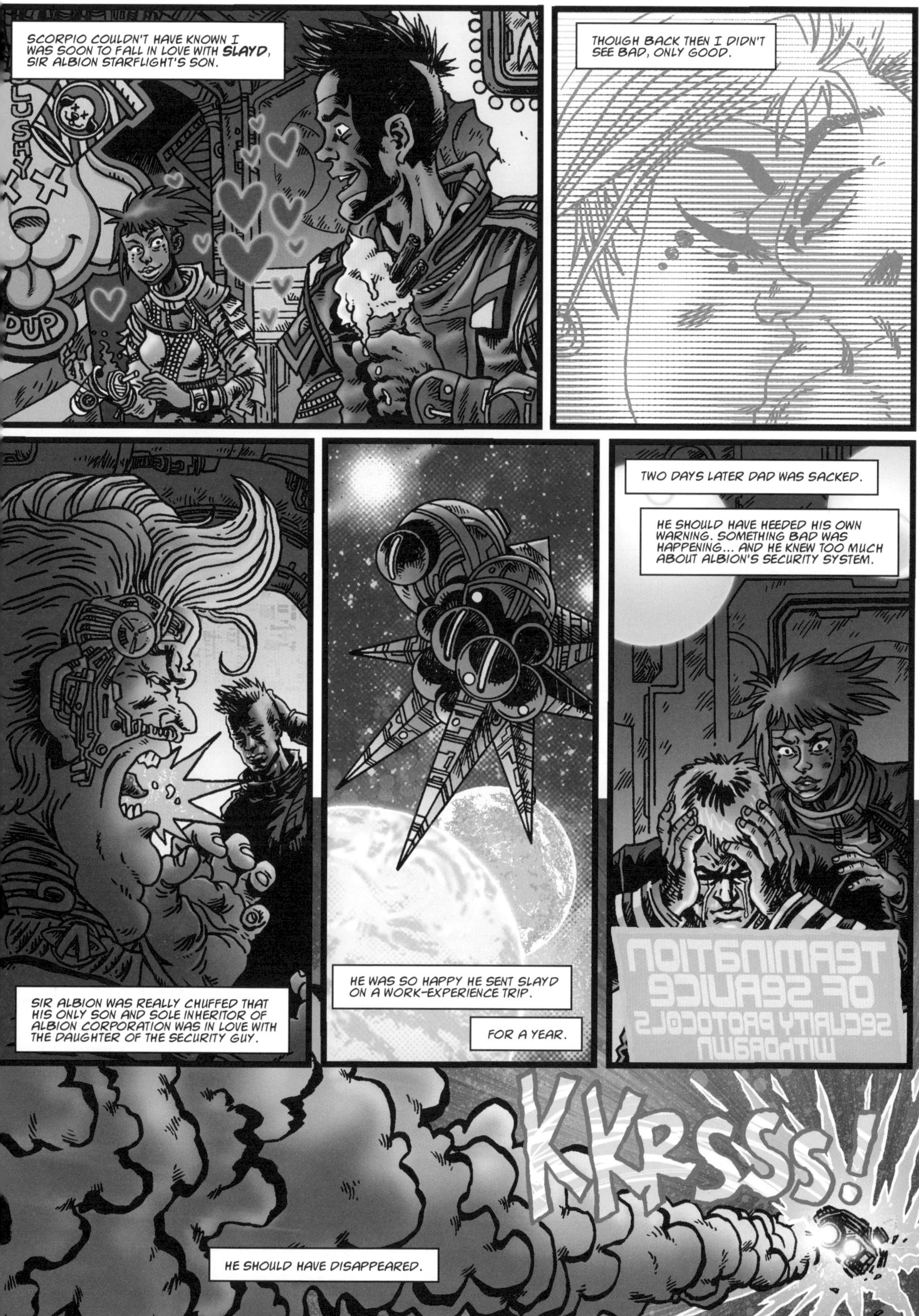
SCORPIO COULDN'T HAVE KNOWN I WAS SOON TO FALL IN LOVE WITH **SLAYD**, SIR ALBION STARFLIGHT'S SON.
THOUGH BACK THEN I DIDN'T SEE BAD, ONLY GOOD.
SIR ALBION WAS REALLY CHUFFED THAT HIS ONLY SON AND SOLE INHERITOR OF ALBION CORPORATION WAS IN LOVE WITH THE DAUGHTER OF THE SECURITY GUY.
HE WAS SO HAPPY HE SENT SLAYD ON A WORK-EXPERIENCE TRIP.
FOR A YEAR.
TWO DAYS LATER DAD WAS SACKED.
HE SHOULD HAVE HEEDED HIS OWN WARNING. SOMETHING BAD WAS HAPPENING... AND HE KNEW TOO MUCH ABOUT ALBION'S SECURITY SYSTEM.
TERMINATION OF SERVICE
SECURITY PROTOCOLS WITHDRAWN
KKRSSS!
HE SHOULD HAVE DISAPPEARED.

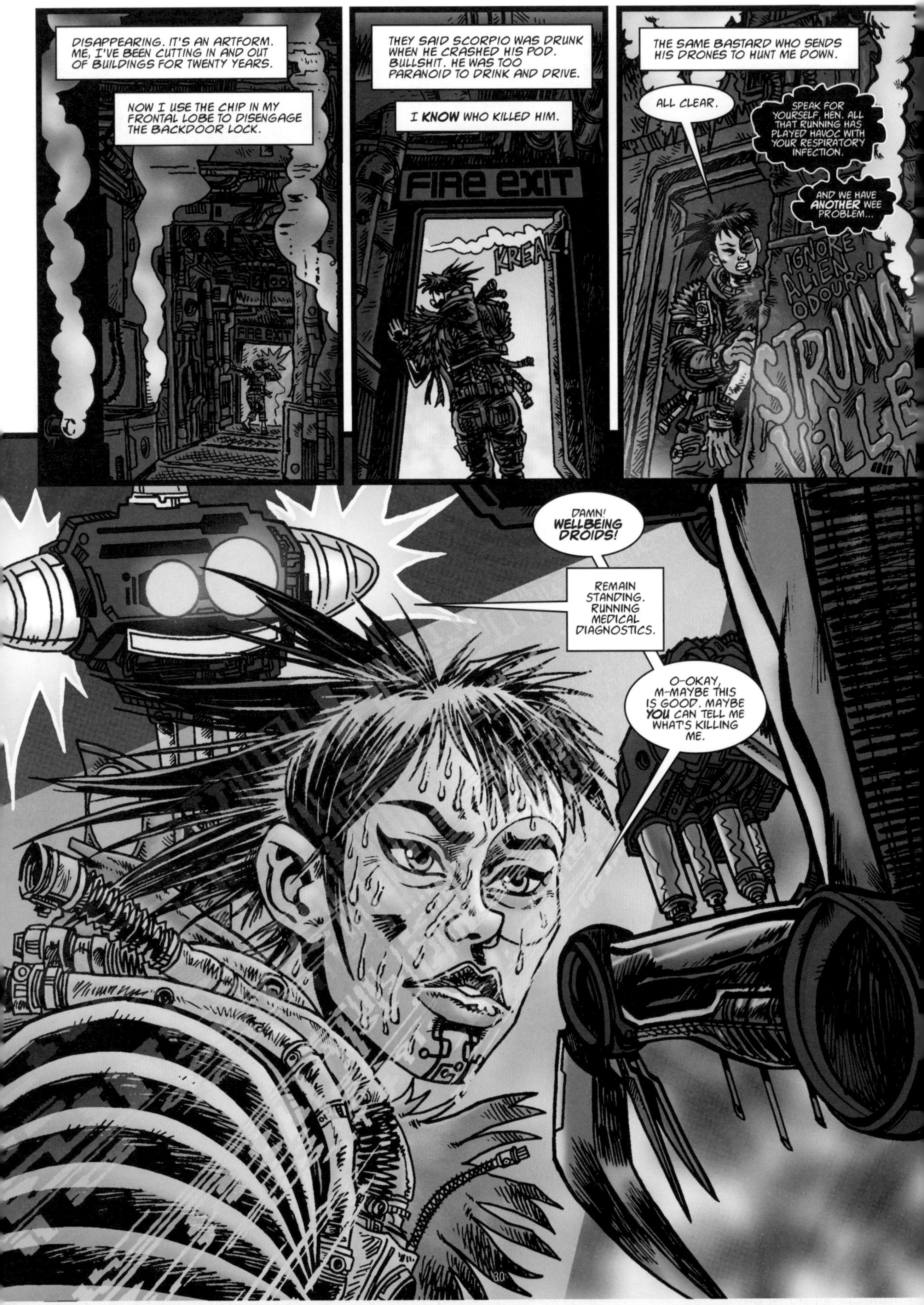
DISAPPEARING. IT'S AN ARTFORM. ME, I'VE BEEN CUTTING IN AND OUT OF BUILDINGS FOR TWENTY YEARS.
NOW I USE THE CHIP IN MY FRONTAL LOBE TO DISENGAGE THE BACKDOOR LOCK.
FIRE EXIT
THEY SAID SCORPIO WAS DRUNK WHEN HE CRASHED HIS POD. BULLSHIT. HE WAS TOO PARANOID TO DRINK AND DRIVE.
I KNOW WHO KILLED HIM.
FIRE EXIT
KREAK
THE SAME BASTARD WHO SENDS HIS DRONES TO HUNT ME DOWN.
ALL CLEAR.
SPEAK FOR YOURSELF, HEN. ALL THAT RUNNING HAS PLAYED HAVOC WITH YOUR RESPIRATORY INFECTION.
AND WE HAVE ANOTHER WEE PROBLEM...
IGNORE ALIEN ODOURS!
STRUM VILLE
DAMN! WELLBEING DROIDS!
REMAIN STANDING. RUNNING MEDICAL DIAGNOSTICS.
O-OKAY, M-MAYBE THIS IS GOOD. MAYBE YOU CAN TELL ME WHAT'S KILLING ME.

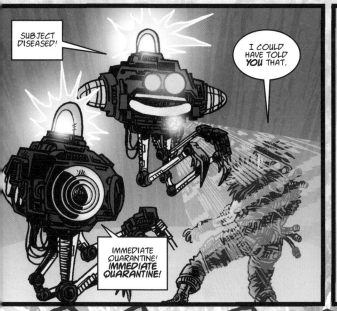

SUBJECT DISEASED!

I COULD HAVE TOLD *YOU* THAT.

IMMEDIATE QUARANTINE! IMMEDIATE QUARANTINE!

QUARANTINE? YOU MEAN LOCKED UP WITH A BUNCH OF SICK PEOPLE? NO THANK YOU —

ZZZZZZZZ

AAAAAHHHHH!

IT'S HARD TO WORRY ABOUT MYSTERY DISEASES OR DODGY PERSONAS OR EVEN ALBION CORPORATION WHEN YOUR BRAIN IS BEING FRIED.

I GUESS THERE'LL BE PLENTY OF TIME FOR WORRYING LATER...

DANGER ELECTRO FENCE

DANGER ELECTRO FENCE

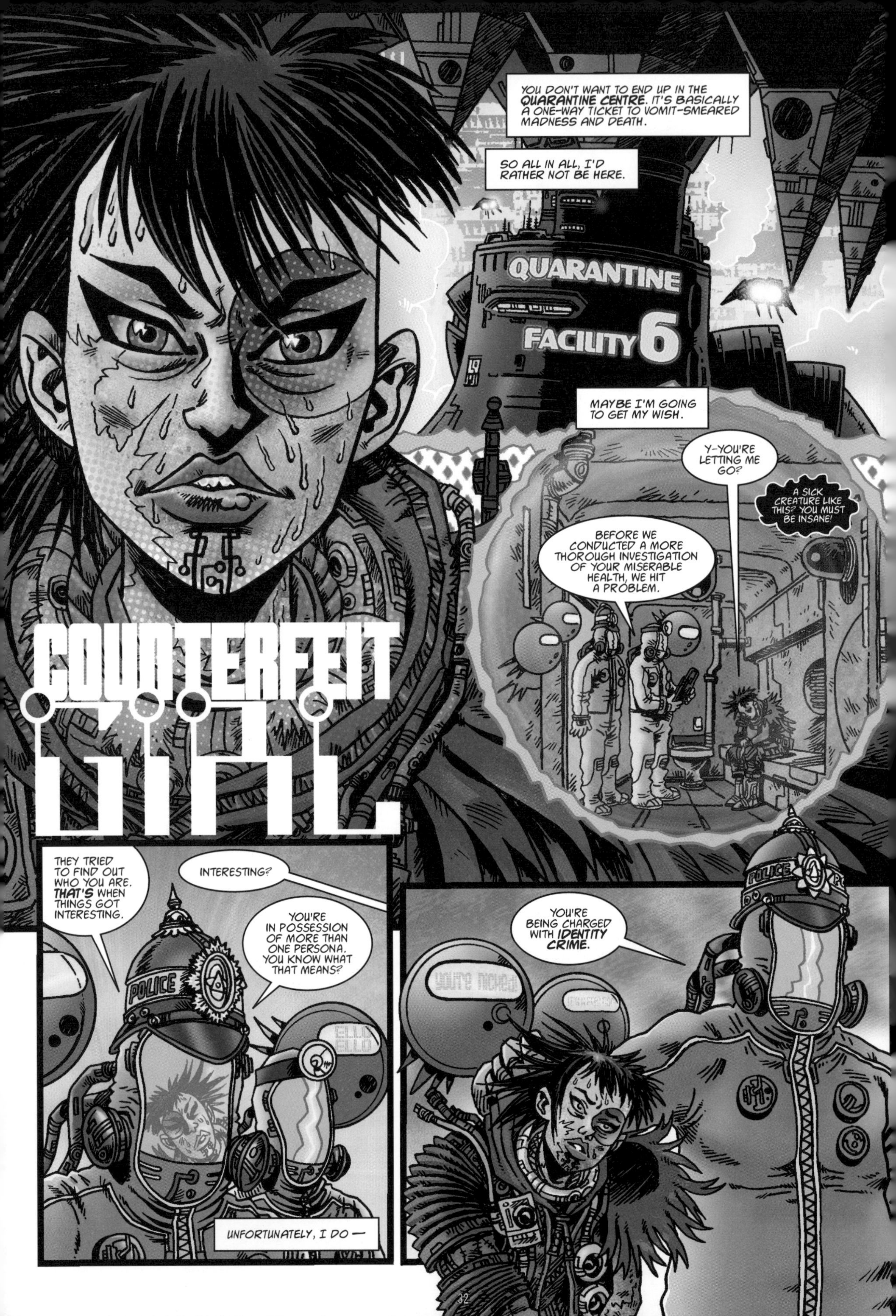
YOU DON'T WANT TO END UP IN THE QUARANTINE CENTRE. IT'S BASICALLY A ONE-WAY TICKET TO VOMIT-SMEARED MADNESS AND DEATH.
SO ALL IN ALL, I'D RATHER NOT BE HERE.
QUARANTINE FACILITY 6
MAYBE I'M GOING TO GET MY WISH.
COUNTERFEIT GIRL
BEFORE WE CONDUCTED A MORE THOROUGH INVESTIGATION OF YOUR MISERABLE HEALTH, WE HIT A PROBLEM.
Y-YOU'RE LETTING ME GO?
A SICK CREATURE LIKE THIS? YOU MUST BE INSANE!
THEY TRIED TO FIND OUT WHO YOU ARE. THAT'S WHEN THINGS GOT INTERESTING.
INTERESTING?
YOU'RE IN POSSESSION OF MORE THAN ONE PERSONA. YOU KNOW WHAT THAT MEANS?
POLICE
ELLO ELLO
UNFORTUNATELY, I DO —
YOU'RE BEING CHARGED WITH IDENTITY CRIME.
YOU'RE NICKED
POLICE

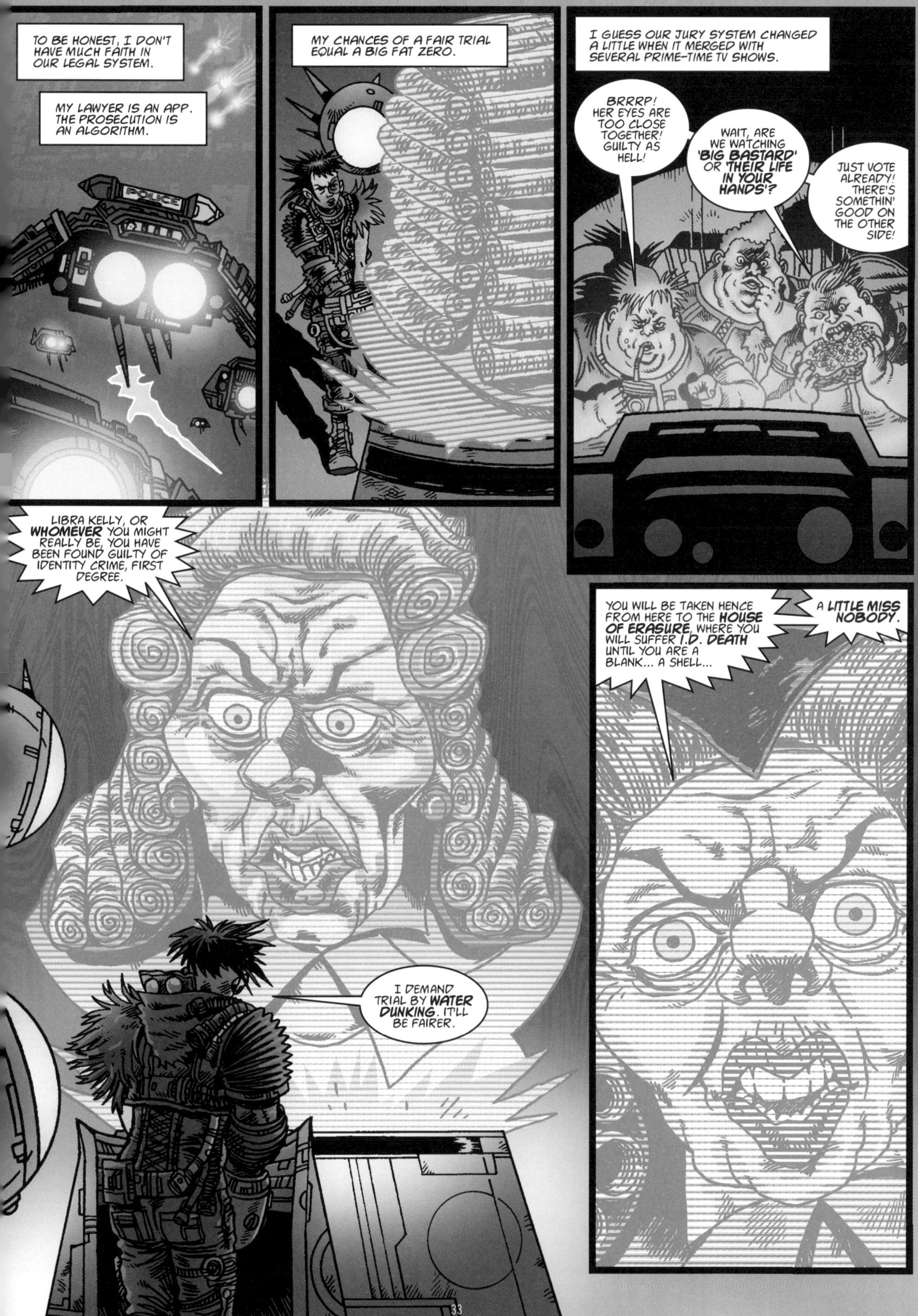

TO BE HONEST, I DON'T HAVE MUCH FAITH IN OUR LEGAL SYSTEM.
MY LAWYER IS AN APP. THE PROSECUTION IS AN ALGORITHM.
POLICE
MY CHANCES OF A FAIR TRIAL EQUAL A BIG FAT ZERO.
I GUESS OUR JURY SYSTEM CHANGED A LITTLE WHEN IT MERGED WITH SEVERAL PRIME-TIME TV SHOWS.
BRRRP! HER EYES ARE TOO CLOSE TOGETHER! GUILTY AS HELL!
WAIT, ARE WE WATCHING 'BIG BASTARD' OR 'THEIR LIFE IN YOUR HANDS'?
JUST VOTE ALREADY! THERE'S SOMETHIN' GOOD ON THE OTHER SIDE!
LIBRA KELLY, OR WHOMEVER YOU MIGHT REALLY BE, YOU HAVE BEEN FOUND GUILTY OF IDENTITY CRIME, FIRST DEGREE.
YOU WILL BE TAKEN HENCE FROM HERE TO THE HOUSE OF ERASURE, WHERE YOU WILL SUFFER I.D. DEATH UNTIL YOU ARE A BLANK... A SHELL...
A LITTLE MISS NOBODY.
I DEMAND TRIAL BY WATER DUNKING. IT'LL BE FAIRER.

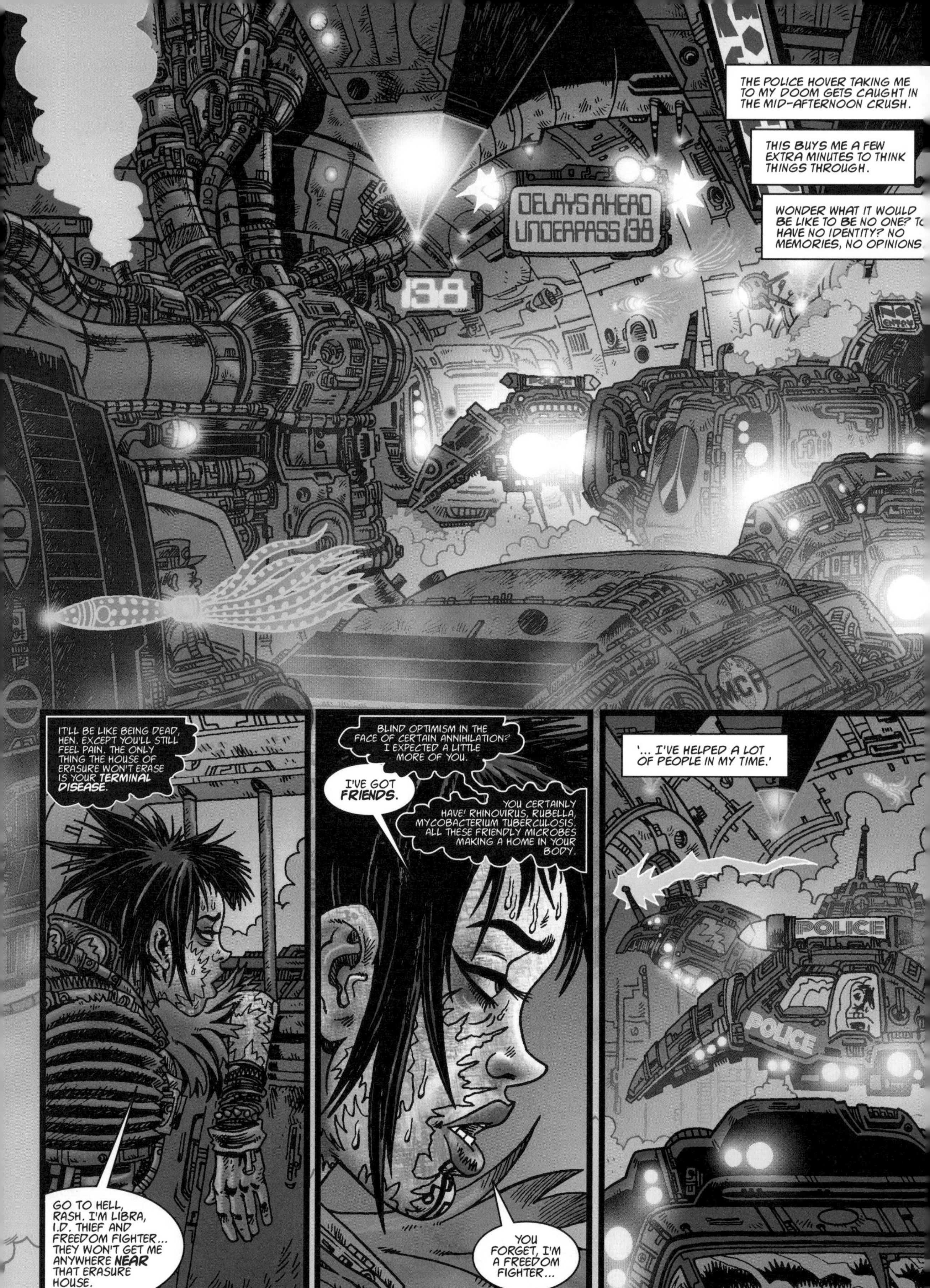

THE POLICE HOVER TAKING ME TO MY DOOM GETS CAUGHT IN THE MID-AFTERNOON CRUSH.
THIS BUYS ME A FEW EXTRA MINUTES TO THINK THINGS THROUGH.
WONDER WHAT IT WOULD BE LIKE TO BE NO ONE? TO HAVE NO IDENTITY? NO MEMORIES, NO OPINIONS.
DELAYS AHEAD UNDERPASS 138
138
POLICE
MCA
IT'LL BE LIKE BEING DEAD, HEN. EXCEPT YOU'LL STILL FEEL PAIN. THE ONLY THING THE HOUSE OF ERASURE WON'T ERASE IS YOUR TERMINAL DISEASE.
GO TO HELL, RASH. I'M LIBRA, I.D. THIEF AND FREEDOM FIGHTER... THEY WON'T GET ME ANYWHERE NEAR THAT ERASURE HOUSE.
BLIND OPTIMISM IN THE FACE OF CERTAIN ANNIHILATION? I EXPECTED A LITTLE MORE OF YOU.
I'VE GOT FRIENDS.
YOU CERTAINLY HAVE! RHINOVIRUS, RUBELLA, MYCOBACTERIUM TUBERCULOSIS. ALL THESE FRIENDLY MICROBES MAKING A HOME IN YOUR BODY.
YOU FORGET, I'M A FREEDOM FIGHTER...
'... I'VE HELPED A LOT OF PEOPLE IN MY TIME.'
POLICE
POLICE

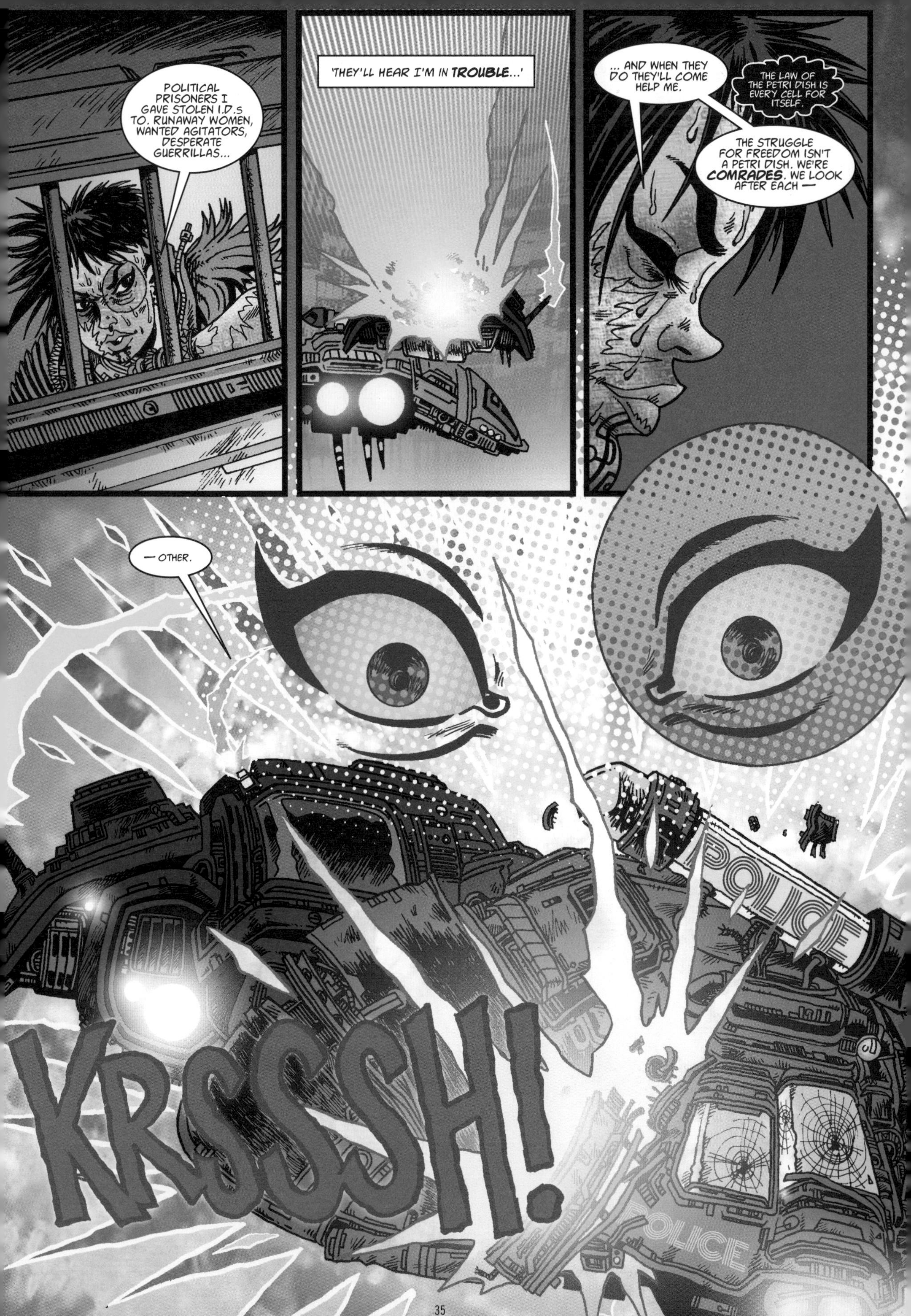
POLITICAL PRISONERS I GAVE STOLEN I.D.s TO. RUNAWAY WOMEN, WANTED AGITATORS, DESPERATE GUERRILLAS...
'THEY'LL HEAR I'M IN TROUBLE...'
... AND WHEN THEY DO THEY'LL COME HELP ME.
THE LAW OF THE PETRI DISH IS EVERY CELL FOR ITSELF.
THE STRUGGLE FOR FREEDOM ISN'T A PETRI DISH. WE'RE COMRADES. WE LOOK AFTER EACH —
— OTHER.
POLICE
KRSSSH!
POLICE

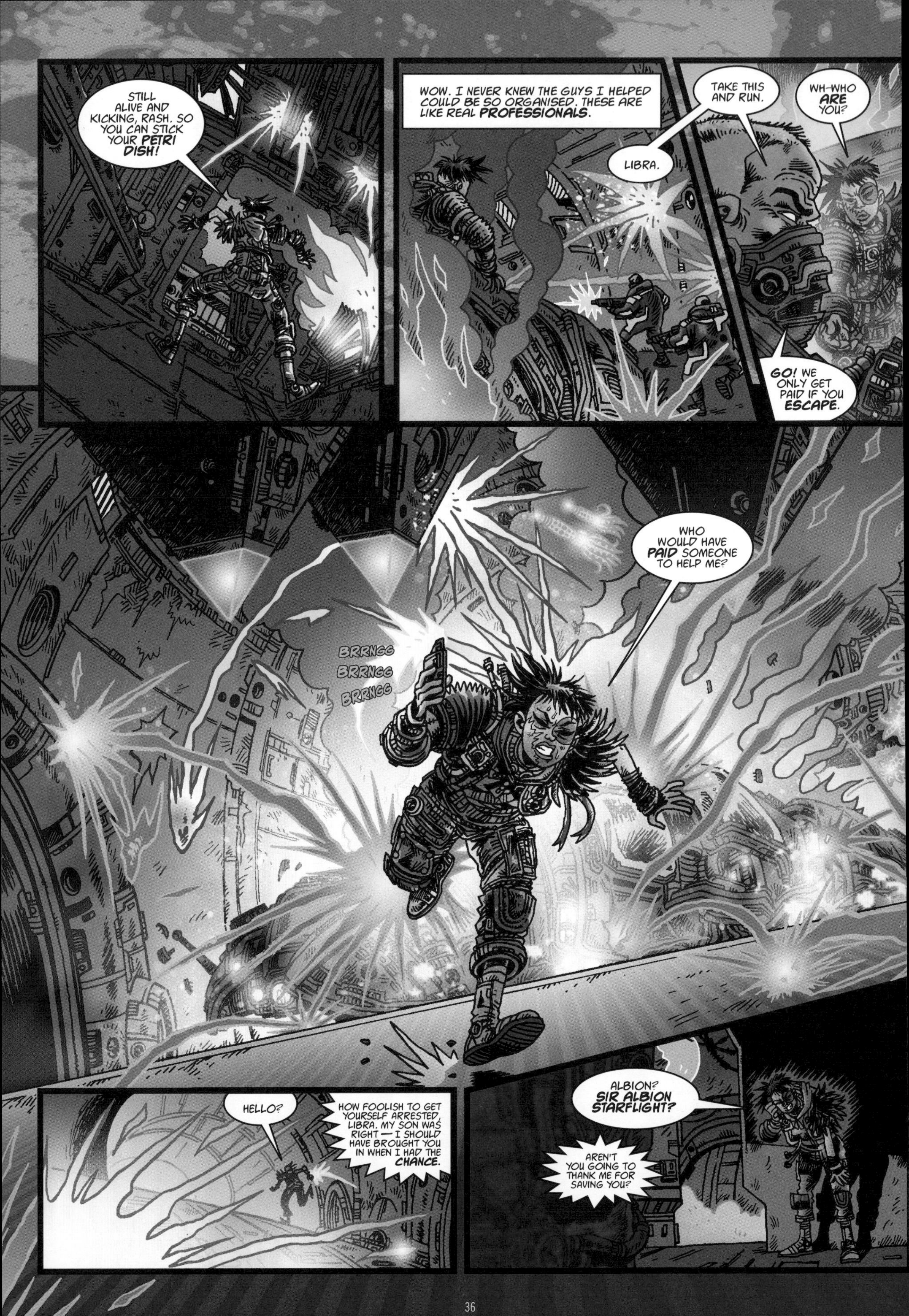

STILL ALIVE AND KICKING, RASH. SO YOU CAN STICK YOUR PETRI DISH!
WOW. I NEVER KNEW THE GUYS I HELPED COULD BE SO ORGANISED. THESE ARE LIKE REAL PROFESSIONALS.
TAKE THIS AND RUN.
LIBRA.
WH-WHO ARE YOU?
GO! WE ONLY GET PAID IF YOU ESCAPE.
WHO WOULD HAVE PAID SOMEONE TO HELP ME?
BRRNGG
BRRNGG
BRRNGG
HELLO?
HOW FOOLISH TO GET YOURSELF ARRESTED, LIBRA. MY SON WAS RIGHT — I SHOULD HAVE BROUGHT YOU IN WHEN I HAD THE CHANCE.
ALBION? SIR ALBION STARFLIGHT?
AREN'T YOU GOING TO THANK ME FOR SAVING YOU?

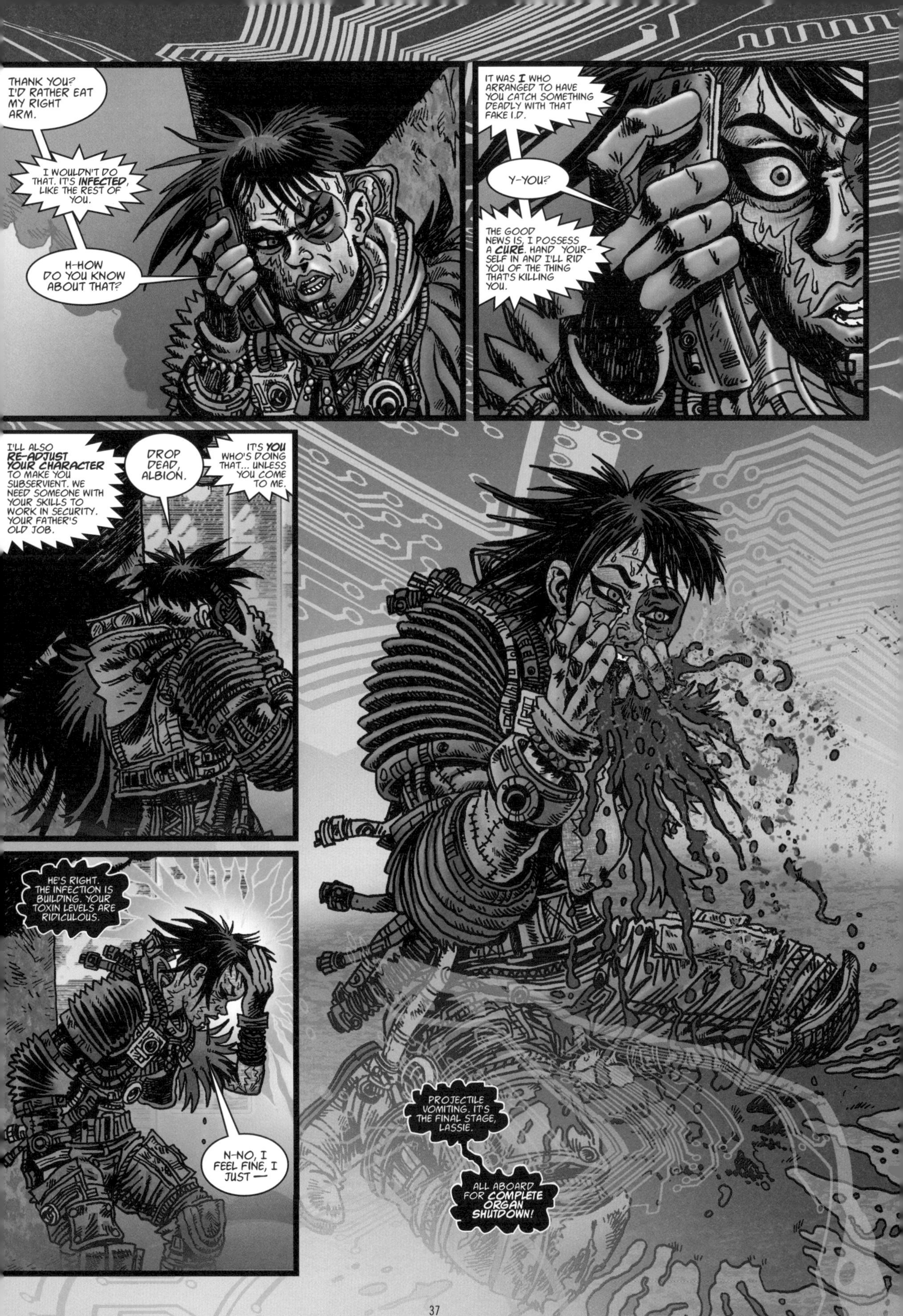

THANK YOU? I'D RATHER EAT MY RIGHT ARM.
I WOULDN'T DO THAT. IT'S INFECTED, LIKE THE REST OF YOU.
H-HOW DO YOU KNOW ABOUT THAT?
IT WAS I WHO ARRANGED TO HAVE YOU CATCH SOMETHING DEADLY WITH THAT FAKE I.D.
Y-YOU?
THE GOOD NEWS IS, I POSSESS A CURE. HAND YOURSELF IN AND I'LL RID YOU OF THE THING THAT'S KILLING YOU.
I'LL ALSO RE-ADJUST YOUR CHARACTER TO MAKE YOU SUBSERVIENT. WE NEED SOMEONE WITH YOUR SKILLS TO WORK IN SECURITY. YOUR FATHER'S OLD JOB.
DROP DEAD, ALBION.
IT'S YOU WHO'S DOING THAT... UNLESS YOU COME TO ME.
HE'S RIGHT. THE INFECTION IS BUILDING. YOUR TOXIN LEVELS ARE RIDICULOUS.
N-NO, I FEEL FINE, I JUST —
PROJECTILE VOMITING. IT'S THE FINAL STAGE, LASSIE.
ALL ABOARD FOR COMPLETE ORGAN SHUTDOWN!

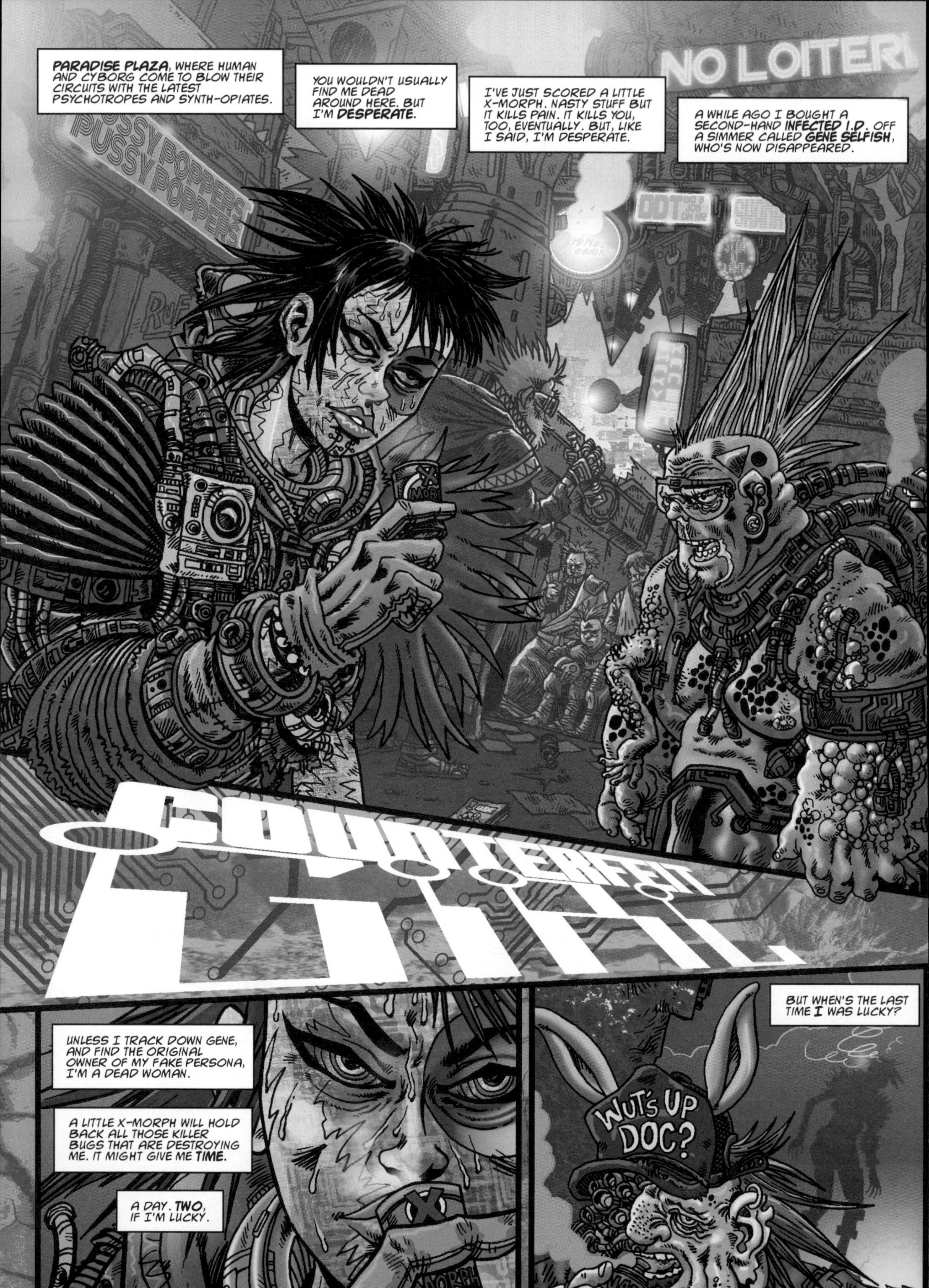

NO LOITERI
PUSSY POPPERS
PUSSY POPPERS
PARADISE PLAZA, WHERE HUMAN AND CYBORG COME TO BLOW THEIR CIRCUITS WITH THE LATEST PSYCHOTROPES AND SYNTH-OPIATES.
YOU WOULDN'T USUALLY FIND ME DEAD AROUND HERE. BUT I'M **DESPERATE**.
I'VE JUST SCORED A LITTLE X-MORPH. NASTY STUFF BUT IT KILLS PAIN. IT KILLS YOU, TOO, EVENTUALLY. BUT, LIKE I SAID, I'M DESPERATE.
A WHILE AGO I BOUGHT A SECOND-HAND **INFECTED I.D.** OFF A SIMMER CALLED **GENE SELFISH**, WHO'S NOW DISAPPEARED.
DDT
COUNTERFEIT
UNLESS I TRACK DOWN GENE, AND FIND THE ORIGINAL OWNER OF MY FAKE PERSONA, I'M A DEAD WOMAN.
A LITTLE X-MORPH WILL HOLD BACK ALL THOSE KILLER BUGS THAT ARE DESTROYING ME. IT MIGHT GIVE ME **TIME**.
A DAY. **TWO**, IF I'M LUCKY.
BUT WHEN'S THE LAST TIME **I** WAS LUCKY?
WUT'S UP DOC?

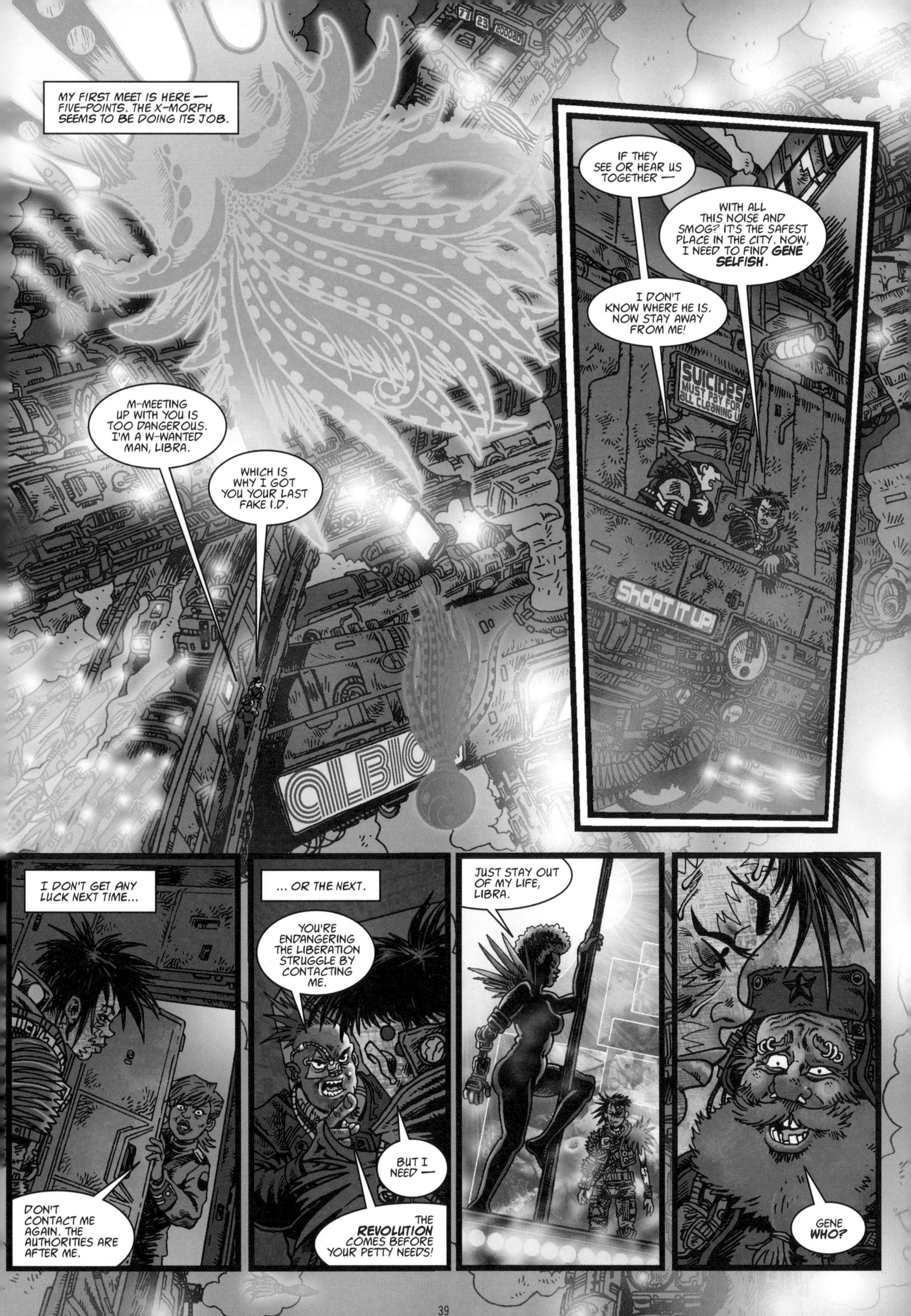
MY FIRST MEET IS HERE — FIVE-POINTS. THE X-MORPH SEEMS TO BE DOING ITS JOB.
M-MEETING UP WITH YOU IS TOO DANGEROUS. I'M A W-WANTED MAN, LIBRA.
WHICH IS WHY I GOT YOU YOUR LAST FAKE I.D.
ALBIO
IF THEY SEE OR HEAR US TOGETHER —
WITH ALL THIS NOISE AND SMOG? IT'S THE SAFEST PLACE IN THE CITY. NOW, I NEED TO FIND **GENE SELFISH**.
I DON'T KNOW WHERE HE IS. NOW STAY AWAY FROM ME!
SUICIDES MUST PAY FOR ALL CLEANING U
SHOOT IT UP!
I DON'T GET ANY LUCK NEXT TIME...
DON'T CONTACT ME AGAIN. THE AUTHORITIES ARE AFTER ME.
... OR THE NEXT.
YOU'RE ENDANGERING THE LIBERATION STRUGGLE BY CONTACTING ME.
BUT I NEED —
THE **REVOLUTION** COMES BEFORE YOUR PETTY NEEDS!
JUST STAY OUT OF MY LIFE, LIBRA.
GENE **WHO?**

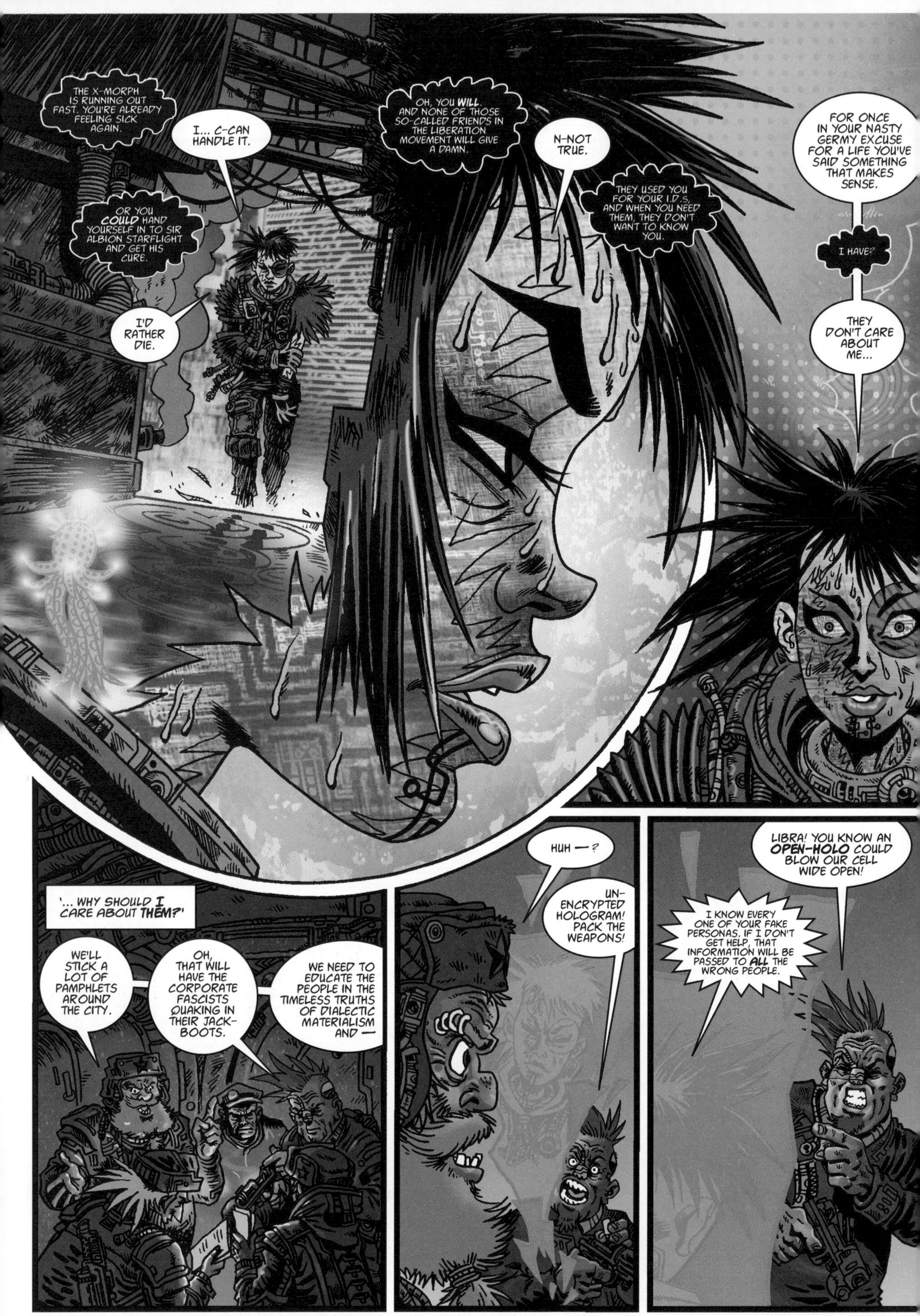
THE X-MORPH IS RUNNING OUT FAST. YOU'RE ALREADY FEELING SICK AGAIN.
I... C-CAN HANDLE IT.
OR YOU COULD HAND YOURSELF IN TO SIR ALBION STARFLIGHT AND GET HIS CURE.
I'D RATHER DIE.
OH, YOU WILL. AND NONE OF THOSE SO-CALLED FRIENDS IN THE LIBERATION MOVEMENT WILL GIVE A DAMN.
N-NOT TRUE.
THEY USED YOU FOR YOUR I.D.S, AND WHEN YOU NEED THEM, THEY DON'T WANT TO KNOW YOU.
FOR ONCE IN YOUR NASTY GERMY EXCUSE FOR A LIFE YOU'VE SAID SOMETHING THAT MAKES SENSE.
I HAVE?
THEY DON'T CARE ABOUT ME...
'... WHY SHOULD I CARE ABOUT THEM?'
WE'LL STICK A LOT OF PAMPHLETS AROUND THE CITY.
OH, THAT WILL HAVE THE CORPORATE FASCISTS QUAKING IN THEIR JACK-BOOTS.
WE NEED TO EDUCATE THE PEOPLE IN THE TIMELESS TRUTHS OF DIALECTIC MATERIALISM AND —
HUH —?
UN-ENCRYPTED HOLOGRAM! PACK THE WEAPONS!
LIBRA! YOU KNOW AN OPEN-HOLO COULD BLOW OUR CELL WIDE OPEN!
I KNOW EVERY ONE OF YOUR FAKE PERSONAS. IF I DON'T GET HELP, THAT INFORMATION WILL BE PASSED TO ALL THE WRONG PEOPLE.

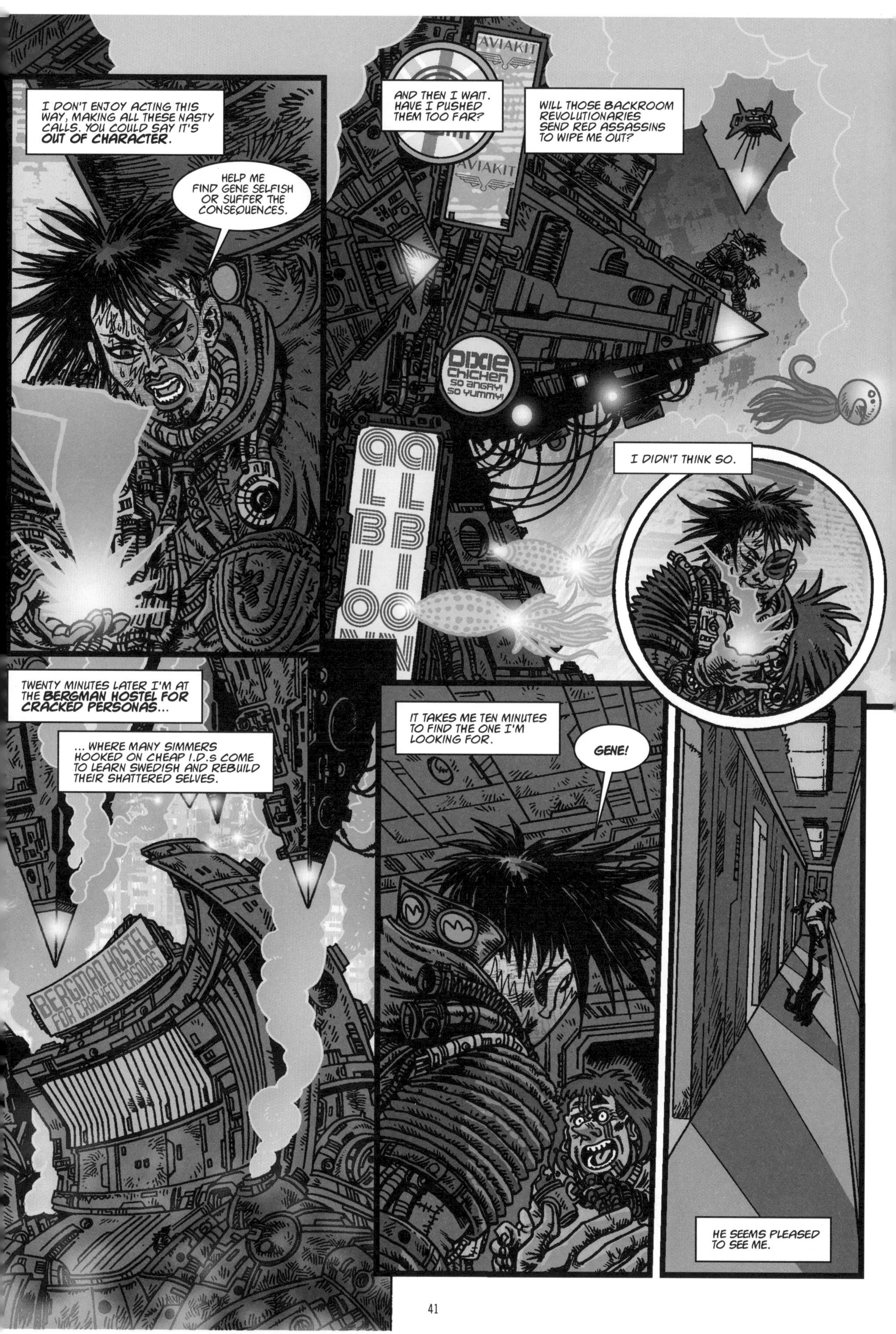
I DON'T ENJOY ACTING THIS WAY, MAKING ALL THESE NASTY CALLS. YOU COULD SAY IT'S **OUT OF CHARACTER**.
HELP ME FIND GENE SELFISH OR SUFFER THE CONSEQUENCES.
AVIAKIT
AND THEN I WAIT. HAVE I PUSHED THEM TOO FAR?
WILL THOSE BACKROOM REVOLUTIONARIES SEND RED ASSASSINS TO WIPE ME OUT?
DIXIE CHICKEN SO ANGRY! SO YUMMY!
I DIDN'T THINK SO.
TWENTY MINUTES LATER I'M AT THE **BERGMAN HOSTEL FOR CRACKED PERSONAS**...
... WHERE MANY SIMMERS HOOKED ON CHEAP I.D.s COME TO LEARN SWEDISH AND REBUILD THEIR SHATTERED SELVES.
BERGMAN HOSTEL FOR CRACKED PERSONAS
IT TAKES ME TEN MINUTES TO FIND THE ONE I'M LOOKING FOR.
GENE!
HE SEEMS PLEASED TO SEE ME.

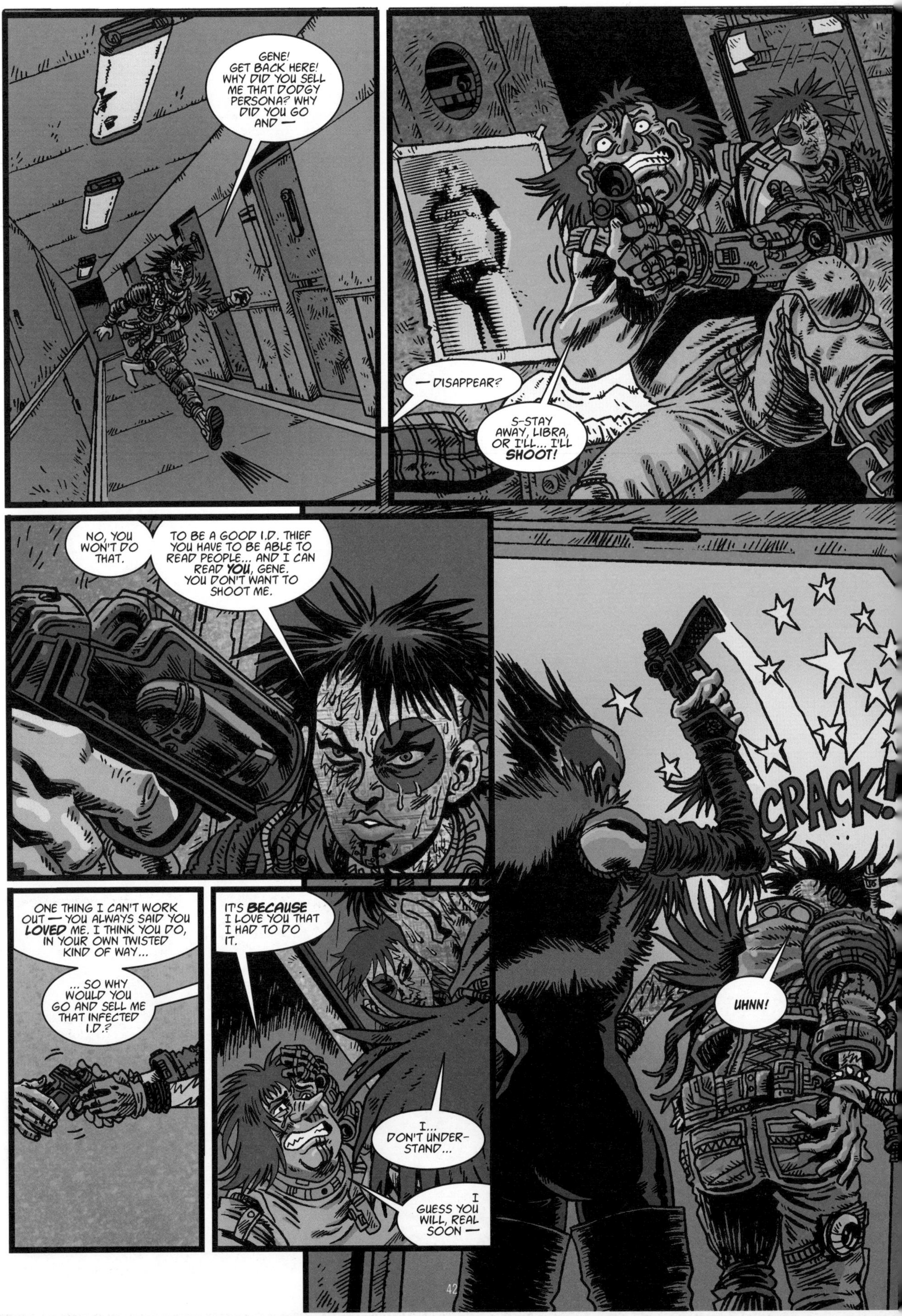
GENE! GET BACK HERE! WHY DID YOU SELL ME THAT DODGY PERSONA? WHY DID YOU GO AND —
— DISAPPEAR?
S-STAY AWAY, LIBRA, OR I'LL... I'LL **SHOOT**!
NO, YOU WON'T DO THAT.
TO BE A GOOD I.D. THIEF YOU HAVE TO BE ABLE TO READ PEOPLE... AND I CAN READ **YOU**, GENE. YOU DON'T WANT TO SHOOT ME.
CRACK!
UHNN!
ONE THING I CAN'T WORK OUT — YOU ALWAYS SAID YOU **LOVED** ME. I THINK YOU DO, IN YOUR OWN TWISTED KIND OF WAY...
... SO WHY WOULD YOU GO AND SELL ME THAT INFECTED I.D.?
IT'S **BECAUSE** I LOVE YOU THAT I HAD TO DO IT.
I... DON'T UNDER-STAND...
I GUESS YOU WILL, REAL SOON —

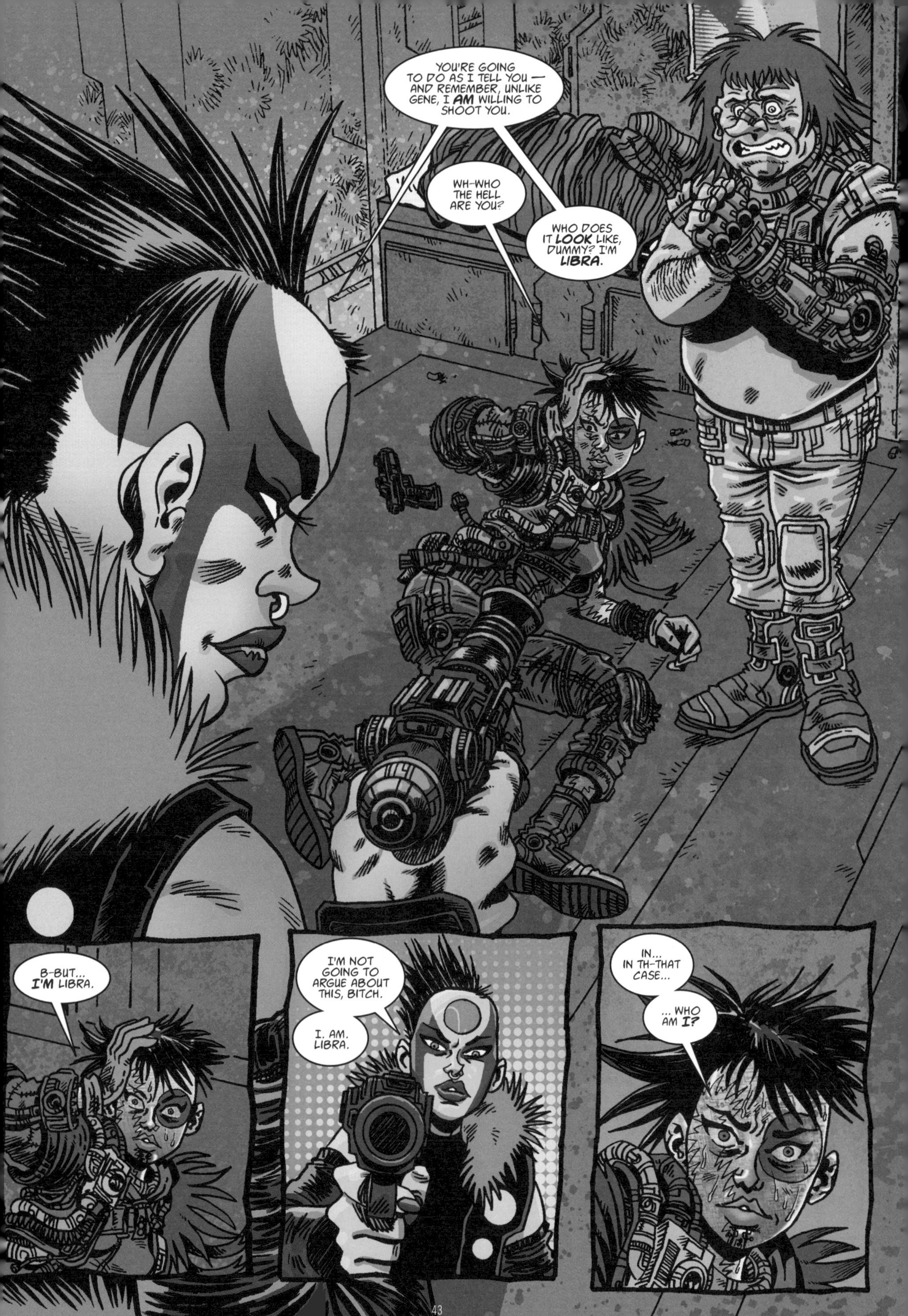
YOU'RE GOING TO DO AS I TELL YOU — AND REMEMBER, UNLIKE GENE, I **AM** WILLING TO SHOOT YOU.
WH-WHO THE HELL ARE YOU?
WHO DOES IT **LOOK** LIKE, DUMMY? I'M **LIBRA**.
B-BUT... **I'M** LIBRA.
I'M NOT GOING TO ARGUE ABOUT THIS, BITCH.
I. AM. LIBRA.
IN... IN TH-THAT CASE...
... WHO AM **I?**

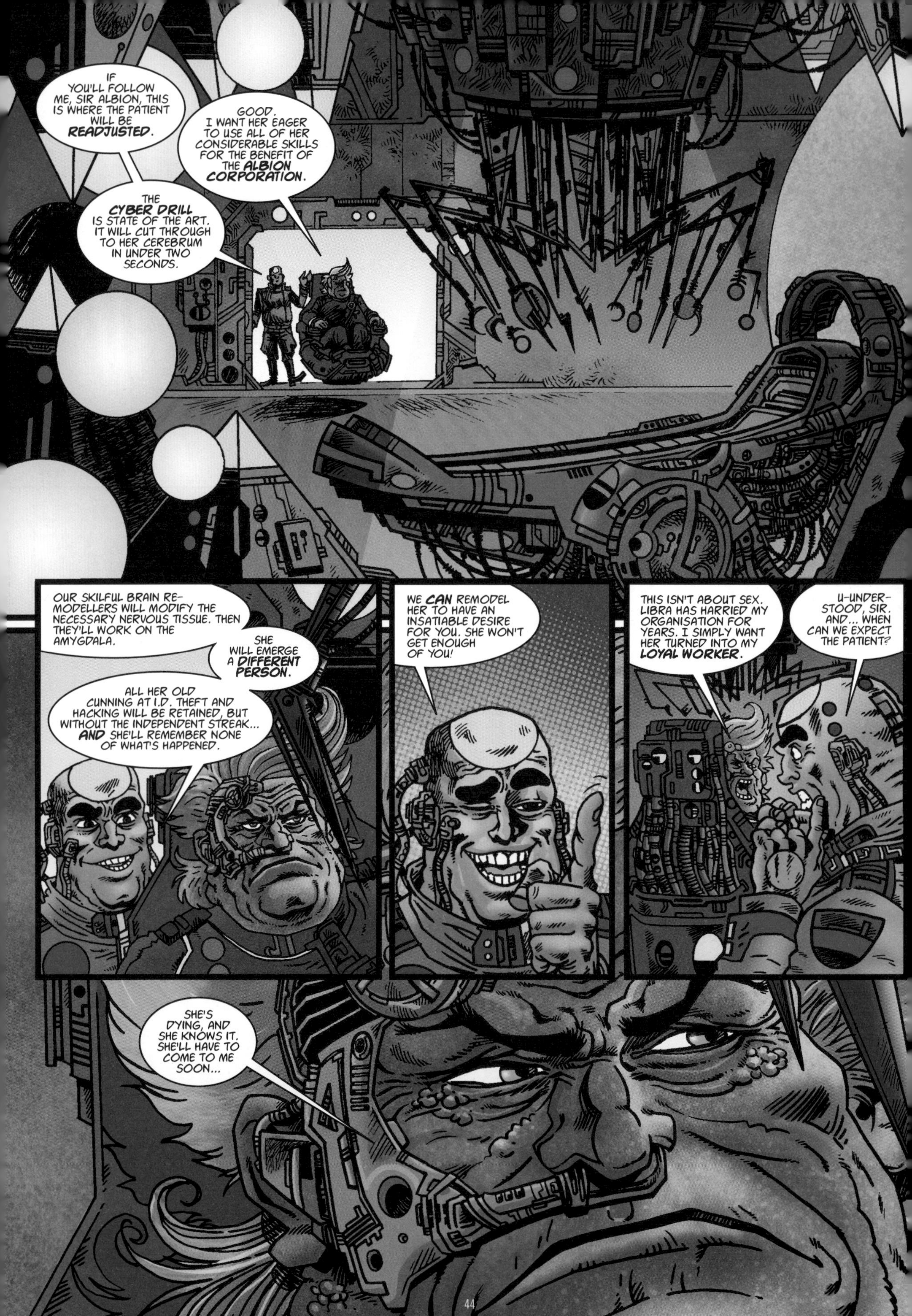
IF YOU'LL FOLLOW ME, SIR ALBION, THIS IS WHERE THE PATIENT WILL BE READJUSTED.
GOOD. I WANT HER EAGER TO USE ALL OF HER CONSIDERABLE SKILLS FOR THE BENEFIT OF THE ALBION CORPORATION.
THE CYBER DRILL IS STATE OF THE ART. IT WILL CUT THROUGH TO HER CEREBRUM IN UNDER TWO SECONDS.
OUR SKILFUL BRAIN RE-MODELLERS WILL MODIFY THE NECESSARY NERVOUS TISSUE. THEN THEY'LL WORK ON THE AMYGDALA.
SHE WILL EMERGE A DIFFERENT PERSON.
ALL HER OLD CUNNING AT I.D. THEFT AND HACKING WILL BE RETAINED, BUT WITHOUT THE INDEPENDENT STREAK... AND SHE'LL REMEMBER NONE OF WHAT'S HAPPENED.
WE CAN REMODEL HER TO HAVE AN INSATIABLE DESIRE FOR YOU. SHE WON'T GET ENOUGH OF YOU!
THIS ISN'T ABOUT SEX. LIBRA HAS HARRIED MY ORGANISATION FOR YEARS. I SIMPLY WANT HER TURNED INTO MY LOYAL WORKER.
U-UNDER-STOOD, SIR. AND... WHEN CAN WE EXPECT THE PATIENT?
SHE'S DYING, AND SHE KNOWS IT. SHE'LL HAVE TO COME TO ME SOON...

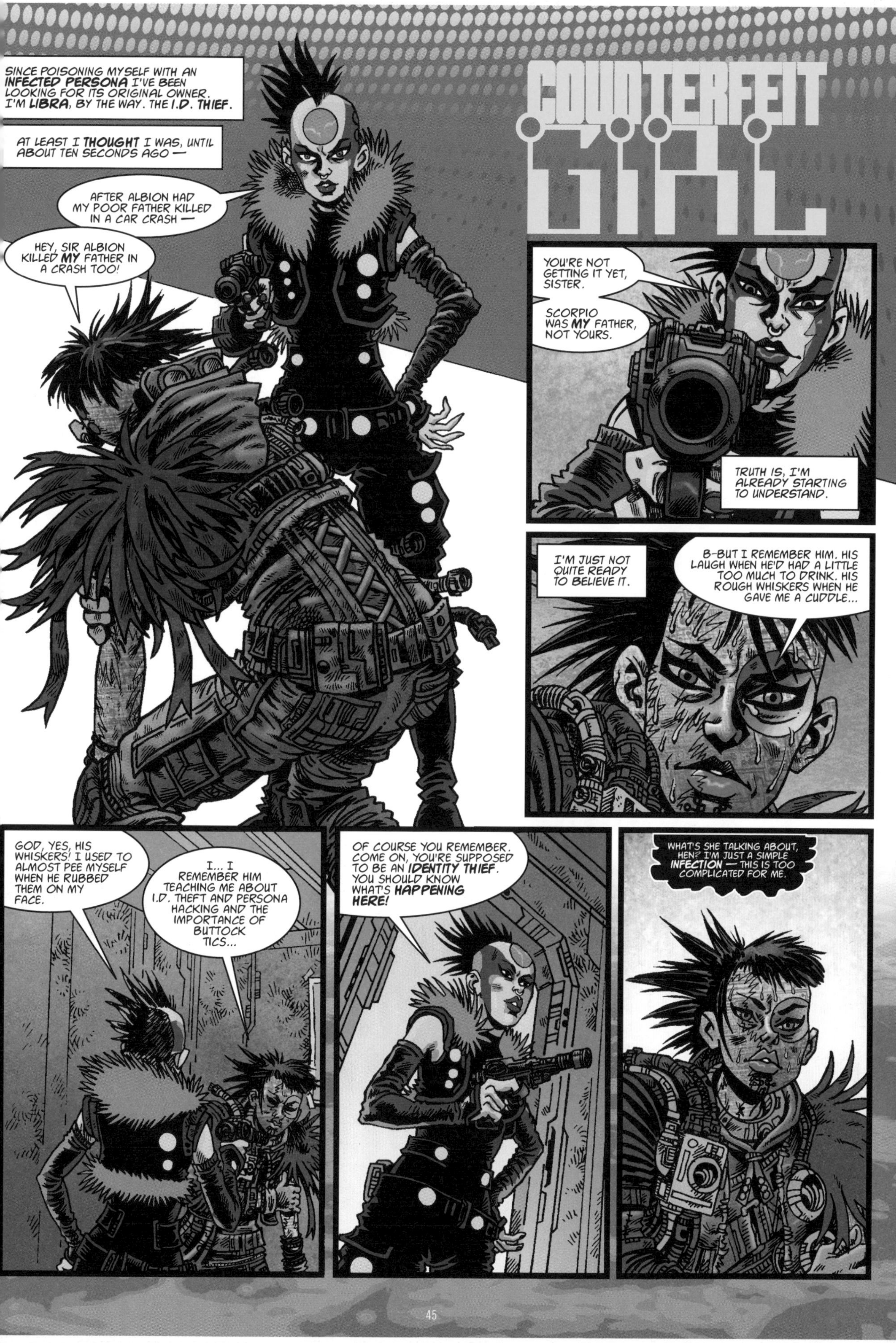

COUNTERFEIT GIRL
SINCE POISONING MYSELF WITH AN INFECTED PERSONA I'VE BEEN LOOKING FOR ITS ORIGINAL OWNER. I'M LIBRA, BY THE WAY. THE I.D. THIEF.
AT LEAST I THOUGHT I WAS, UNTIL ABOUT TEN SECONDS AGO —
AFTER ALBION HAD MY POOR FATHER KILLED IN A CAR CRASH —
HEY, SIR ALBION KILLED MY FATHER IN A CRASH TOO!
YOU'RE NOT GETTING IT YET, SISTER.
SCORPIO WAS MY FATHER, NOT YOURS.
TRUTH IS, I'M ALREADY STARTING TO UNDERSTAND.
I'M JUST NOT QUITE READY TO BELIEVE IT.
B-BUT I REMEMBER HIM. HIS LAUGH WHEN HE'D HAD A LITTLE TOO MUCH TO DRINK. HIS ROUGH WHISKERS WHEN HE GAVE ME A CUDDLE...
GOD, YES, HIS WHISKERS! I USED TO ALMOST PEE MYSELF WHEN HE RUBBED THEM ON MY FACE.
I... I REMEMBER HIM TEACHING ME ABOUT I.D. THEFT AND PERSONA HACKING AND THE IMPORTANCE OF BUTTOCK TICS...
OF COURSE YOU REMEMBER. COME ON, YOU'RE SUPPOSED TO BE AN IDENTITY THIEF. YOU SHOULD KNOW WHAT'S HAPPENING HERE!
WHAT'S SHE TALKING ABOUT, HEN? I'M JUST A SIMPLE INFECTION — THIS IS TOO COMPLICATED FOR ME.

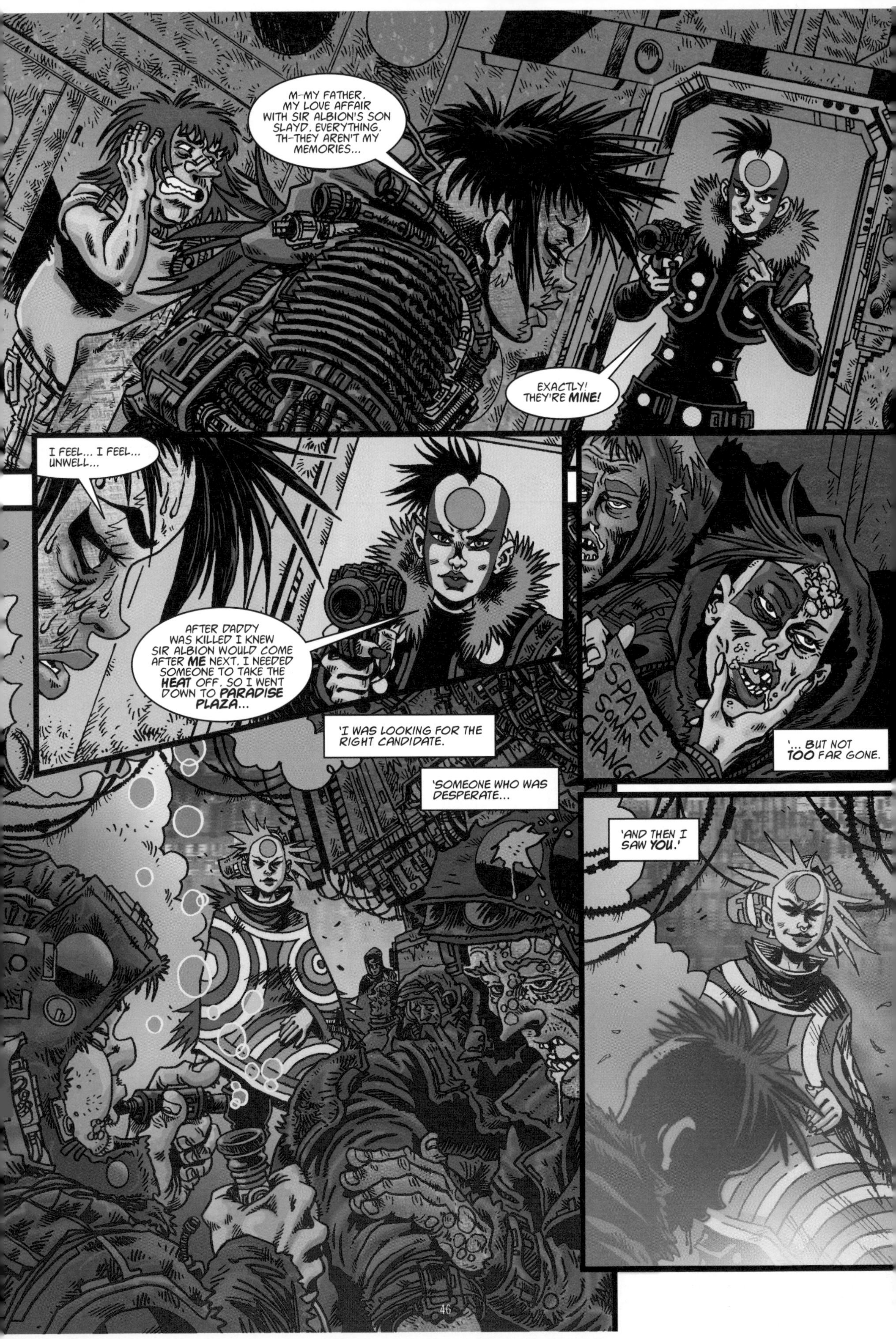
M-MY FATHER. MY LOVE AFFAIR WITH SIR ALBION'S SON SLAYD. EVERYTHING. TH-THEY AREN'T MY MEMORIES...
EXACTLY! THEY'RE **MINE!**
I FEEL... I FEEL... UNWELL...
AFTER DADDY WAS KILLED I KNEW SIR ALBION WOULD COME AFTER **ME** NEXT. I NEEDED SOMEONE TO TAKE THE **HEAT** OFF. SO I WENT DOWN TO **PARADISE PLAZA**...
'I WAS LOOKING FOR THE RIGHT CANDIDATE.
'SOMEONE WHO WAS DESPERATE...
SPARE SOMM CHANGE
'... BUT NOT **TOO** FAR GONE.
'AND THEN I SAW **YOU**.'

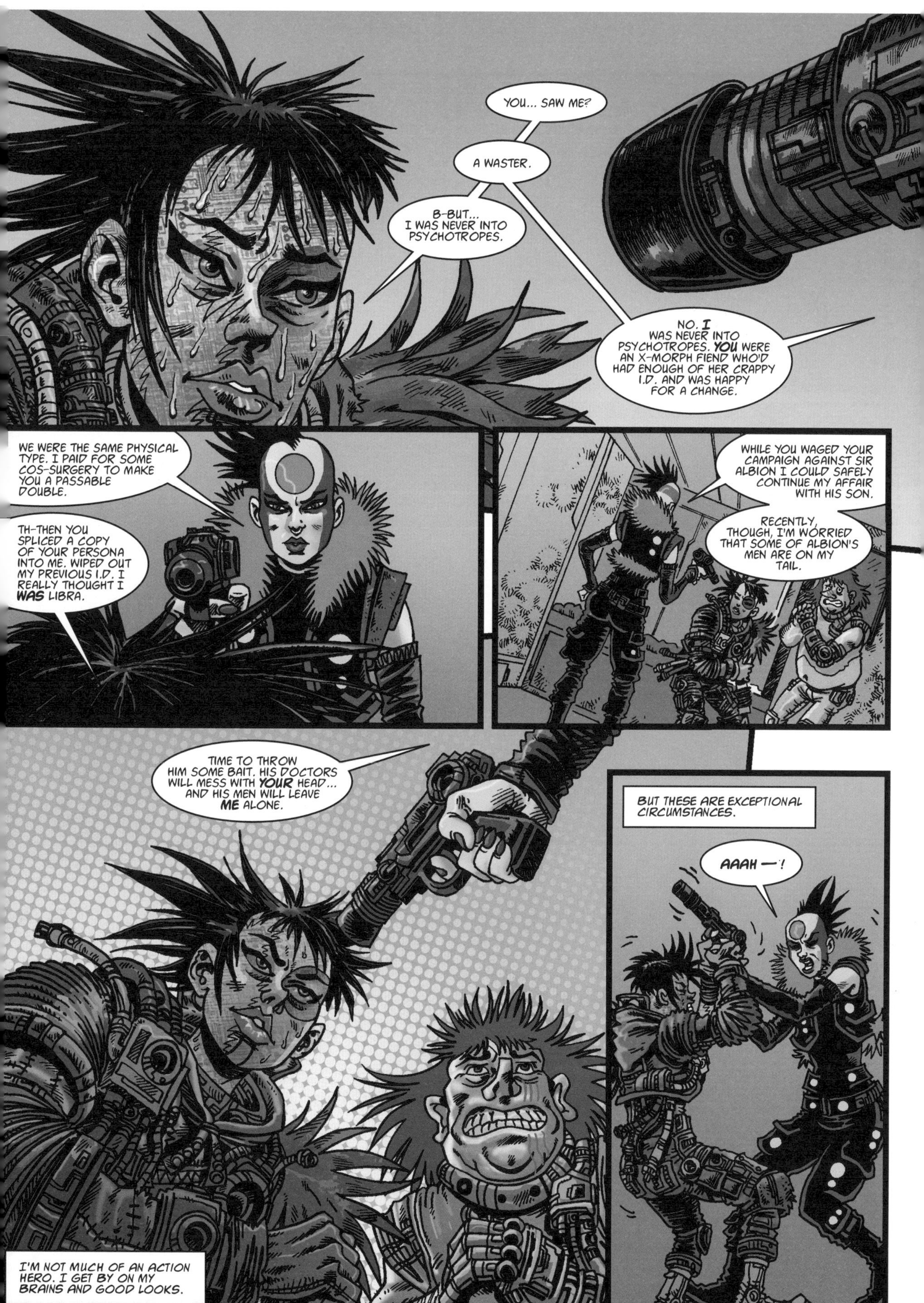
YOU... SAW ME?
A WASTER.
B-BUT... I WAS NEVER INTO PSYCHOTROPES.
NO. I WAS NEVER INTO PSYCHOTROPES. YOU WERE AN X-MORPH FIEND WHO'D HAD ENOUGH OF HER CRAPPY I.D. AND WAS HAPPY FOR A CHANGE.
WE WERE THE SAME PHYSICAL TYPE. I PAID FOR SOME COS-SURGERY TO MAKE YOU A PASSABLE DOUBLE.
TH-THEN YOU SPLICED A COPY OF YOUR PERSONA INTO ME. WIPED OUT MY PREVIOUS I.D. I REALLY THOUGHT I WAS LIBRA.
WHILE YOU WAGED YOUR CAMPAIGN AGAINST SIR ALBION I COULD SAFELY CONTINUE MY AFFAIR WITH HIS SON.
RECENTLY, THOUGH, I'M WORRIED THAT SOME OF ALBION'S MEN ARE ON MY TAIL.
TIME TO THROW HIM SOME BAIT. HIS DOCTORS WILL MESS WITH YOUR HEAD... AND HIS MEN WILL LEAVE ME ALONE.
BUT THESE ARE EXCEPTIONAL CIRCUMSTANCES.
AAAH —!
I'M NOT MUCH OF AN ACTION HERO. I GET BY ON MY BRAINS AND GOOD LOOKS.
R.I.P. STEVE DILLON ♥

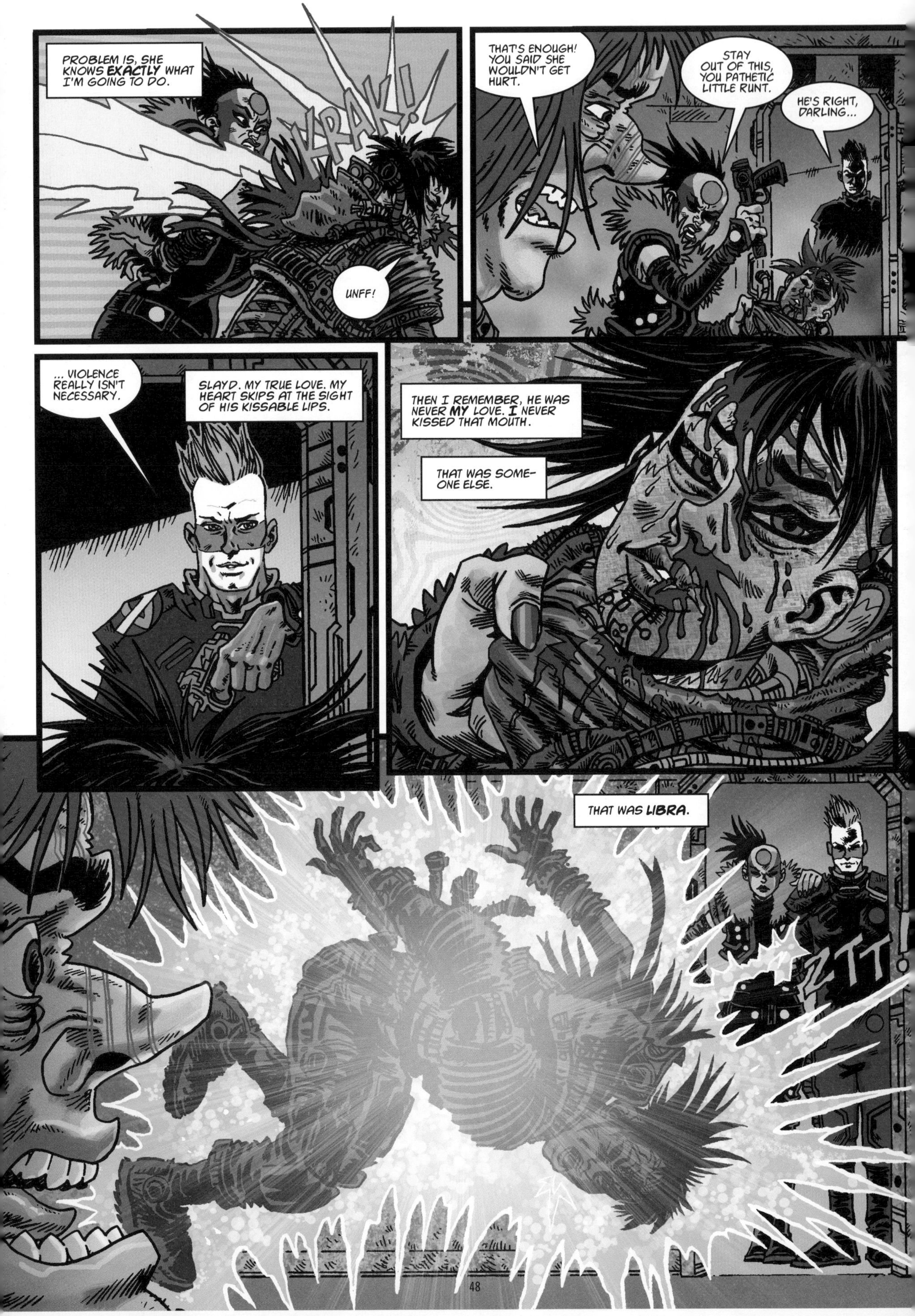
PROBLEM IS, SHE KNOWS EXACTLY WHAT I'M GOING TO DO.
KRAK!
UNFF!
THAT'S ENOUGH! YOU SAID SHE WOULDN'T GET HURT.
STAY OUT OF THIS, YOU PATHETIC LITTLE RUNT.
HE'S RIGHT, DARLING...
... VIOLENCE REALLY ISN'T NECESSARY.
SLAYD. MY TRUE LOVE. MY HEART SKIPS AT THE SIGHT OF HIS KISSABLE LIPS.
THEN I REMEMBER, HE WAS NEVER MY LOVE. I NEVER KISSED THAT MOUTH.
THAT WAS SOME-ONE ELSE.
THAT WAS LIBRA.
ZTT

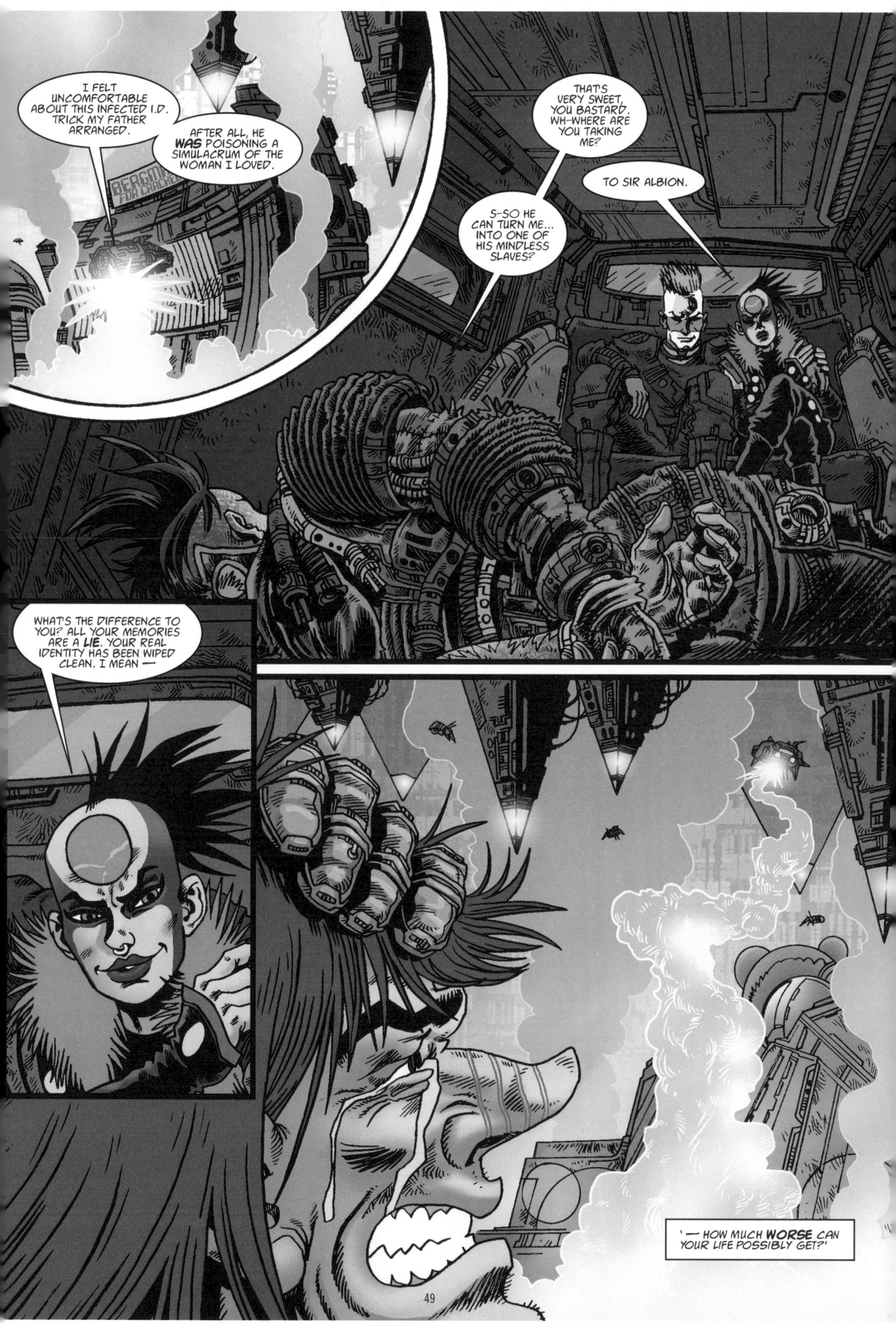
I FELT UNCOMFORTABLE ABOUT THIS INFECTED I.D. TRICK MY FATHER ARRANGED.
AFTER ALL, HE **WAS** POISONING A SIMULACRUM OF THE WOMAN I LOVED.
THAT'S VERY SWEET, YOU BASTARD. WH-WHERE ARE YOU TAKING ME?
TO SIR ALBION.
S-SO HE CAN TURN ME... INTO ONE OF HIS MINDLESS SLAVES?
WHAT'S THE DIFFERENCE TO YOU? ALL YOUR MEMORIES ARE A **LIE**. YOUR REAL IDENTITY HAS BEEN WIPED CLEAN. I MEAN —
'— HOW MUCH **WORSE** CAN YOUR LIFE POSSIBLY GET?'

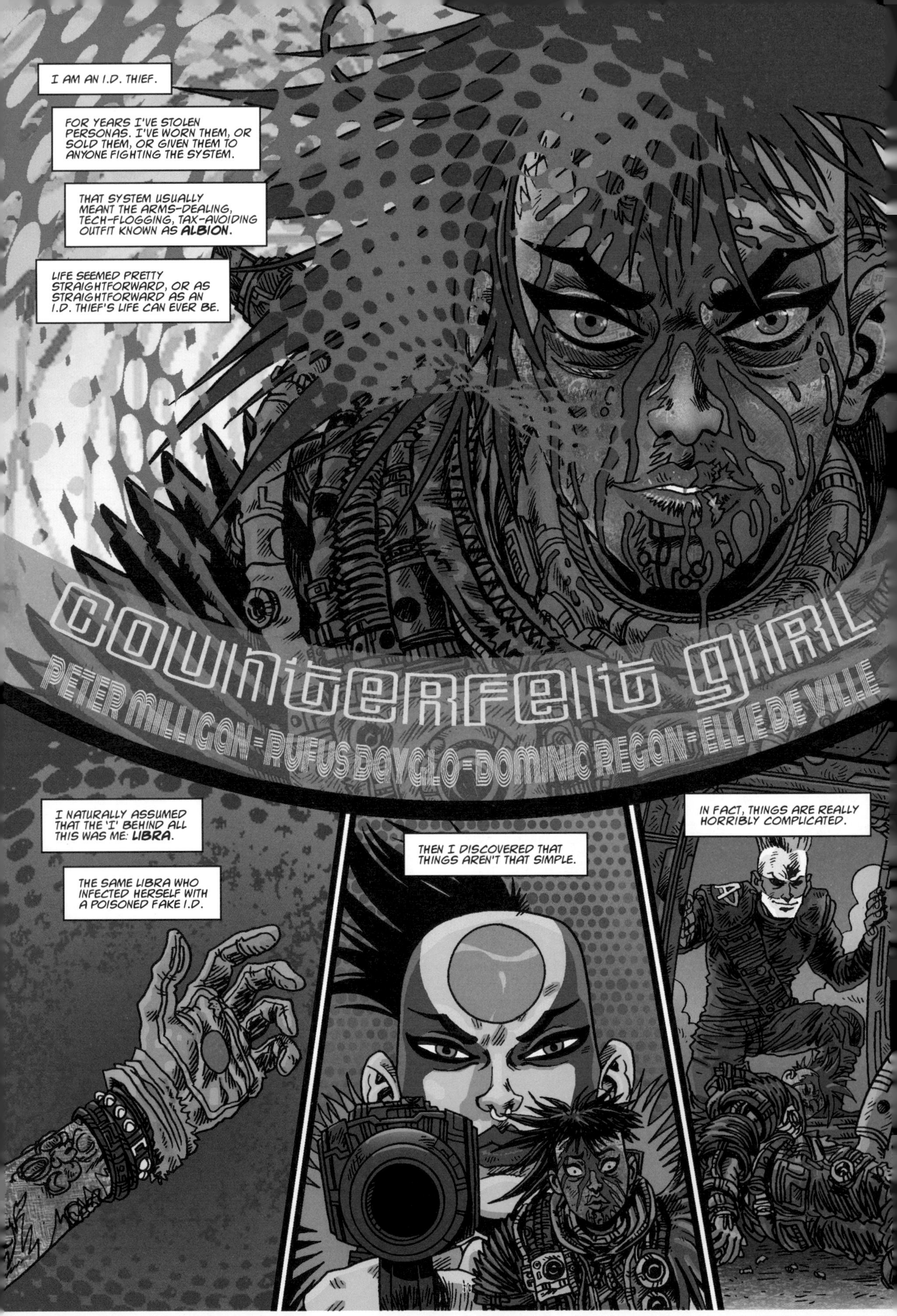
I AM AN I.D. THIEF.
FOR YEARS I'VE STOLEN PERSONAS. I'VE WORN THEM, OR SOLD THEM, OR GIVEN THEM TO ANYONE FIGHTING THE SYSTEM.
THAT SYSTEM USUALLY MEANT THE ARMS-DEALING, TECH-FLOGGING, TAX-AVOIDING OUTFIT KNOWN AS **ALBION**.
LIFE SEEMED PRETTY STRAIGHTFORWARD, OR AS STRAIGHTFORWARD AS AN I.D. THIEF'S LIFE CAN EVER BE.
COUNTERFEIT GIRL
PETER MILLIGAN = RUFUS DAYGLO = DOMINIC REGAN = ELLIE DE VILLE
I NATURALLY ASSUMED THAT THE 'I' BEHIND ALL THIS WAS ME: **LIBRA**.
THE SAME LIBRA WHO INFECTED HERSELF WITH A POISONED FAKE I.D.
THEN I DISCOVERED THAT THINGS AREN'T THAT SIMPLE.
IN FACT, THINGS ARE REALLY HORRIBLY COMPLICATED.

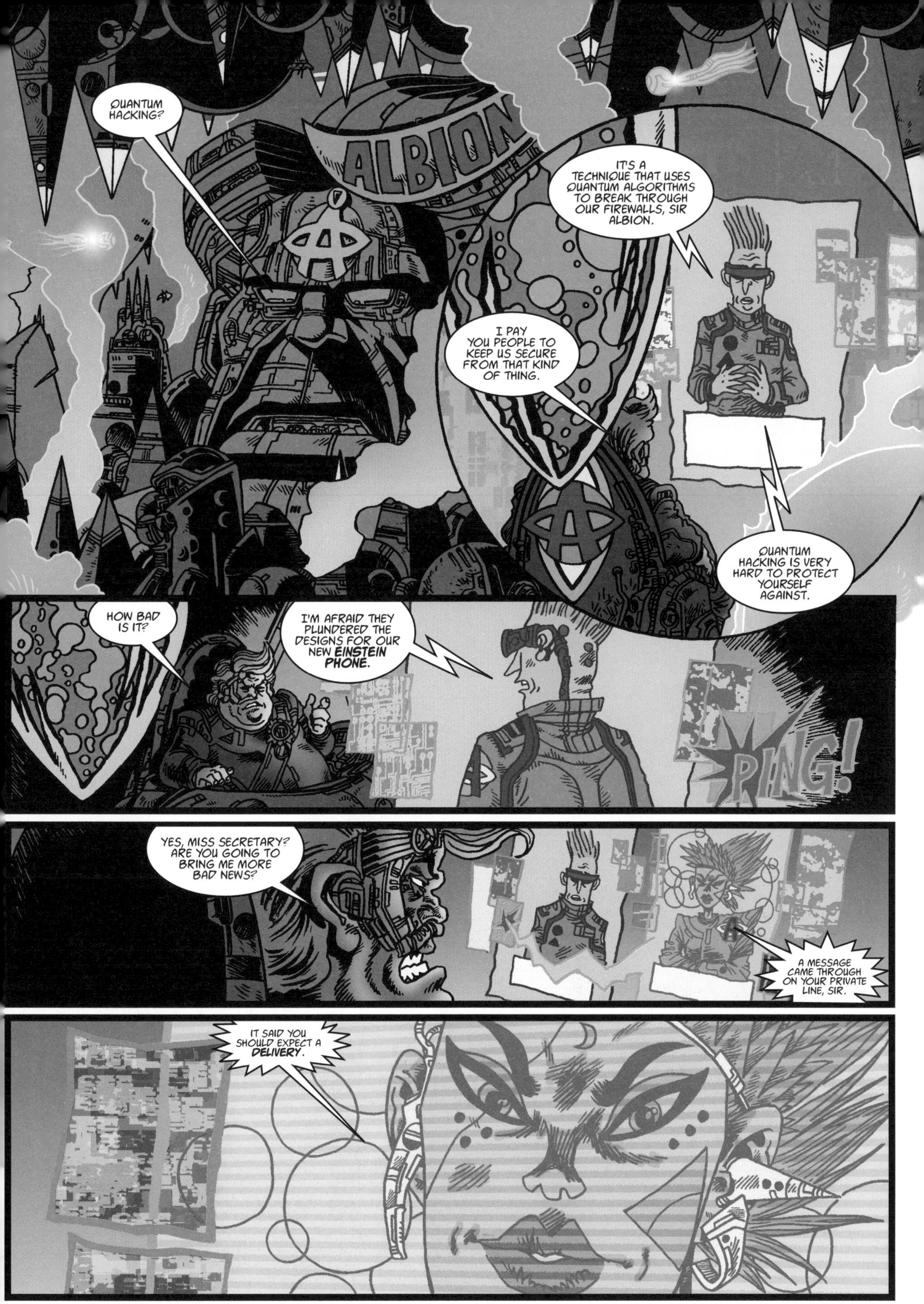

QUANTUM HACKING?
ALBION
IT'S A TECHNIQUE THAT USES QUANTUM ALGORITHMS TO BREAK THROUGH OUR FIREWALLS, SIR ALBION.
I PAY YOU PEOPLE TO KEEP US SECURE FROM THAT KIND OF THING.
QUANTUM HACKING IS VERY HARD TO PROTECT YOURSELF AGAINST.
HOW BAD IS IT?
I'M AFRAID THEY PLUNDERED THE DESIGNS FOR OUR NEW **EINSTEIN PHONE**.
PING!
YES, MISS SECRETARY? ARE YOU GOING TO BRING ME MORE BAD NEWS?
A MESSAGE CAME THROUGH ON YOUR PRIVATE LINE, SIR.
IT SAID YOU SHOULD EXPECT A **DELIVERY**.

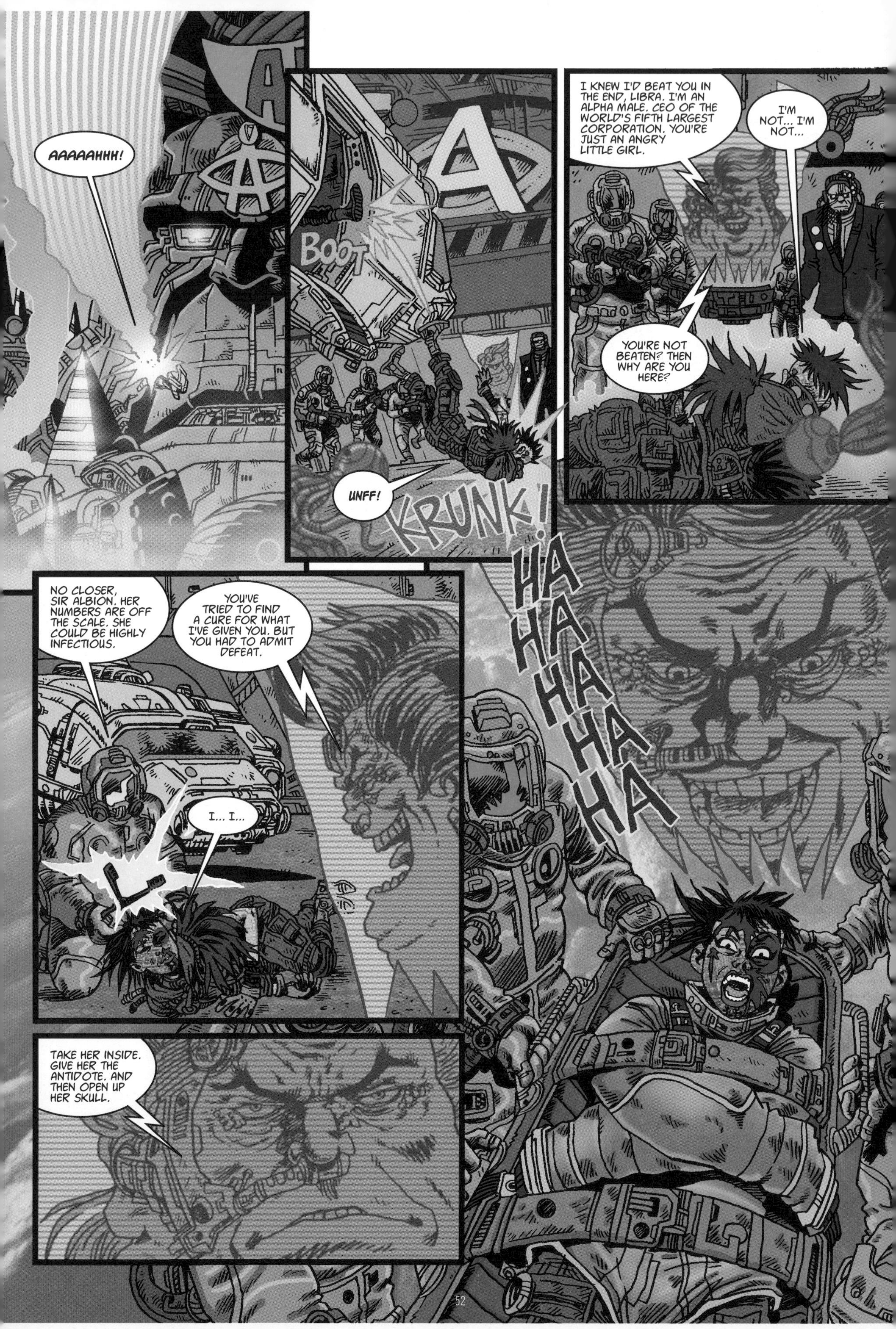
AAAAAHHH!
BOOT
UNFF!
KRUNK!
I KNEW I'D BEAT YOU IN THE END, LIBRA. I'M AN ALPHA MALE. CEO OF THE WORLD'S FIFTH LARGEST CORPORATION. YOU'RE JUST AN ANGRY LITTLE GIRL.
I'M NOT... I'M NOT...
YOU'RE NOT BEATEN? THEN WHY ARE YOU HERE?
NO CLOSER, SIR ALBION. HER NUMBERS ARE OFF THE SCALE. SHE COULD BE HIGHLY INFECTIOUS.
YOU'VE TRIED TO FIND A CURE FOR WHAT I'VE GIVEN YOU. BUT YOU HAD TO ADMIT DEFEAT.
I... I...
HA HA HA HA HA HA HA HA
TAKE HER INSIDE. GIVE HER THE ANTIDOTE. AND THEN OPEN UP HER SKULL.

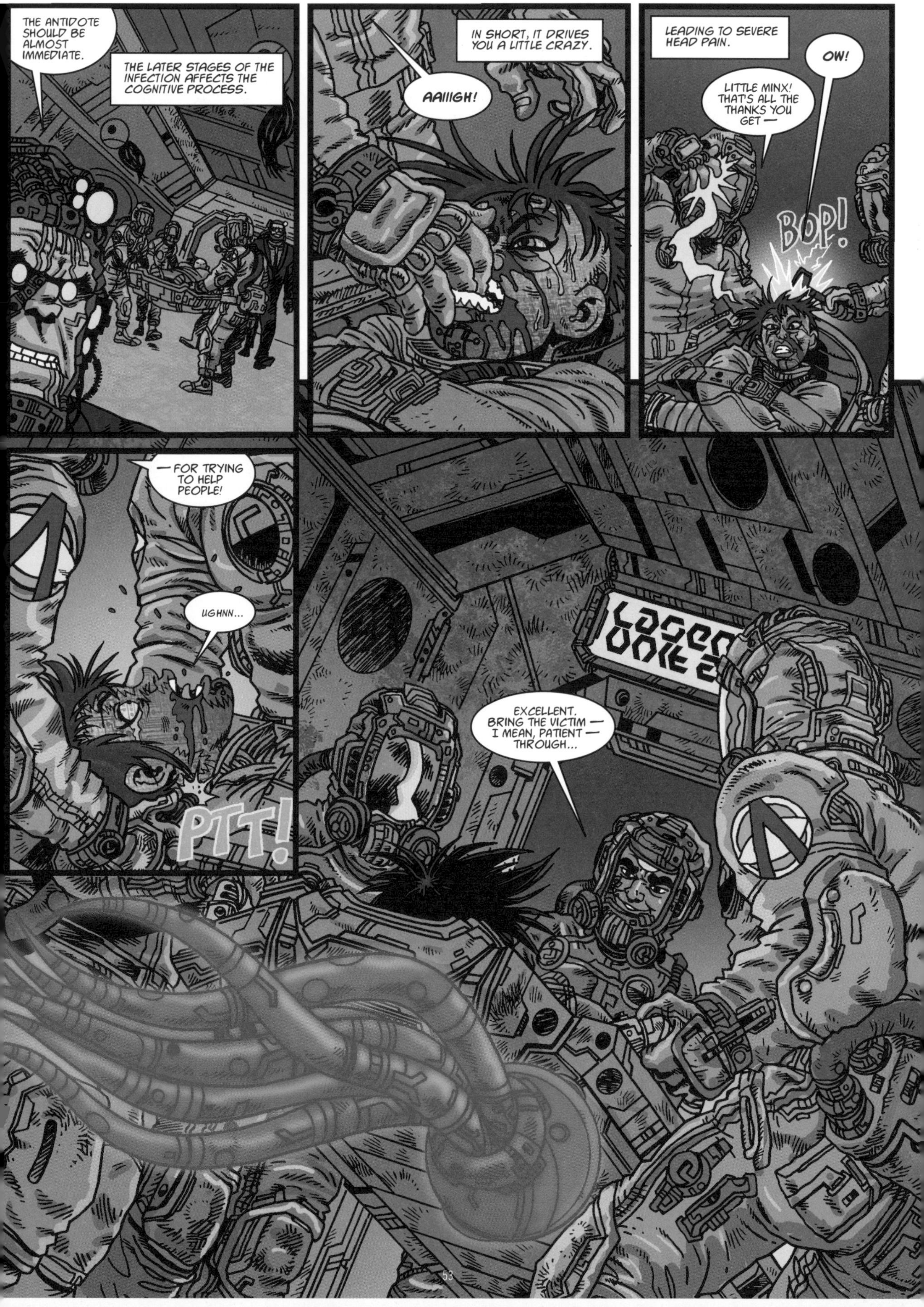
THE ANTIDOTE SHOULD BE ALMOST IMMEDIATE.
THE LATER STAGES OF THE INFECTION AFFECTS THE COGNITIVE PROCESS.
IN SHORT, IT DRIVES YOU A LITTLE CRAZY.
AAIIIGH!
LEADING TO SEVERE HEAD PAIN.
OW!
LITTLE MINX! THAT'S ALL THE THANKS YOU GET —
BOP!
— FOR TRYING TO HELP PEOPLE!
UGHNN...
PTT!
EXCELLENT. BRING THE VICTIM — I MEAN, PATIENT — THROUGH...

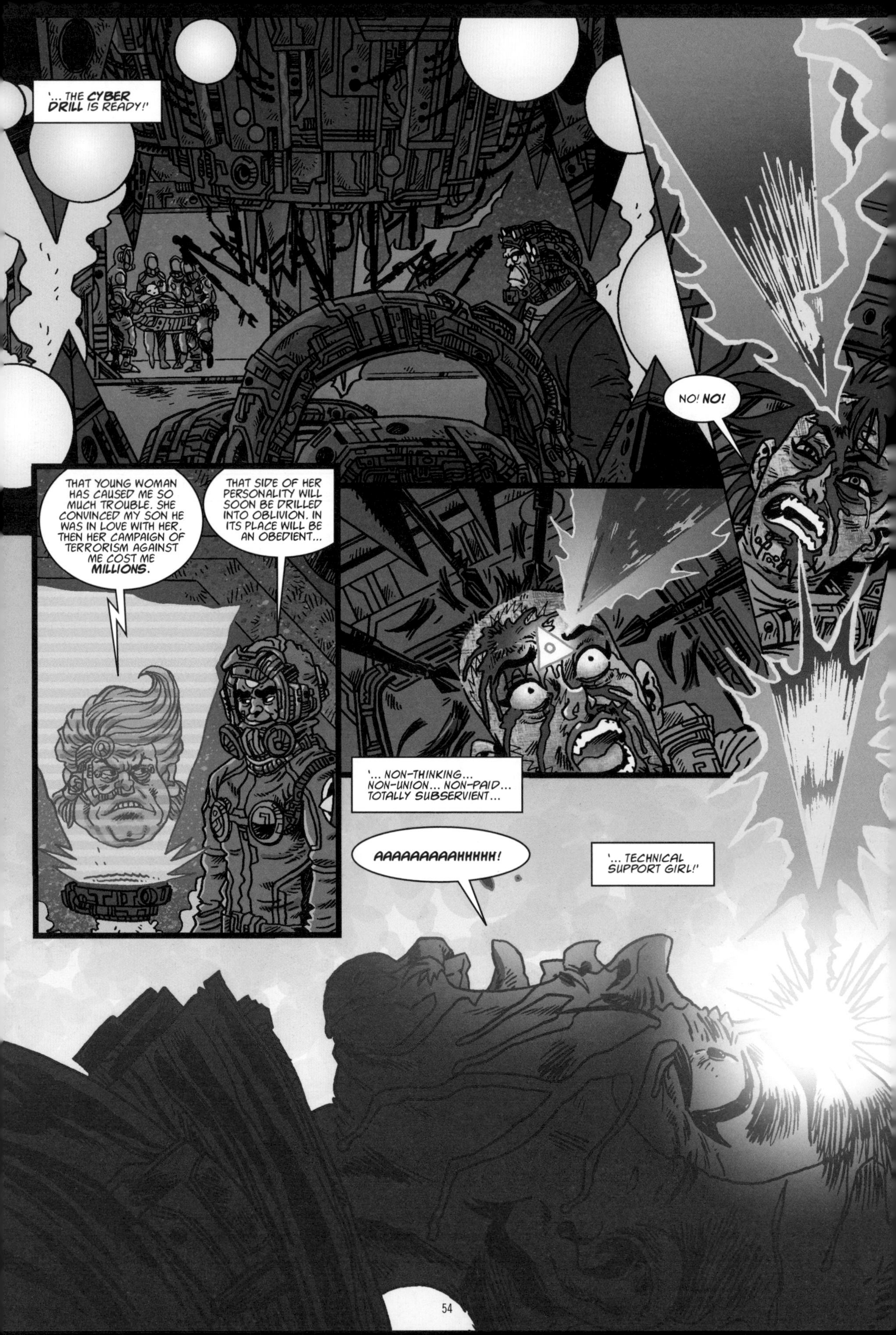
'... THE CYBER DRILL IS READY!'
NO! NO!
THAT YOUNG WOMAN HAS CAUSED ME SO MUCH TROUBLE. SHE CONVINCED MY SON HE WAS IN LOVE WITH HER. THEN HER CAMPAIGN OF TERRORISM AGAINST ME COST ME MILLIONS.
THAT SIDE OF HER PERSONALITY WILL SOON BE DRILLED INTO OBLIVION. IN ITS PLACE WILL BE AN OBEDIENT...
'... NON-THINKING... NON-UNION... NON-PAID... TOTALLY SUBSERVIENT...
AAAAAAAAAHHHHH!
'... TECHNICAL SUPPORT GIRL!'

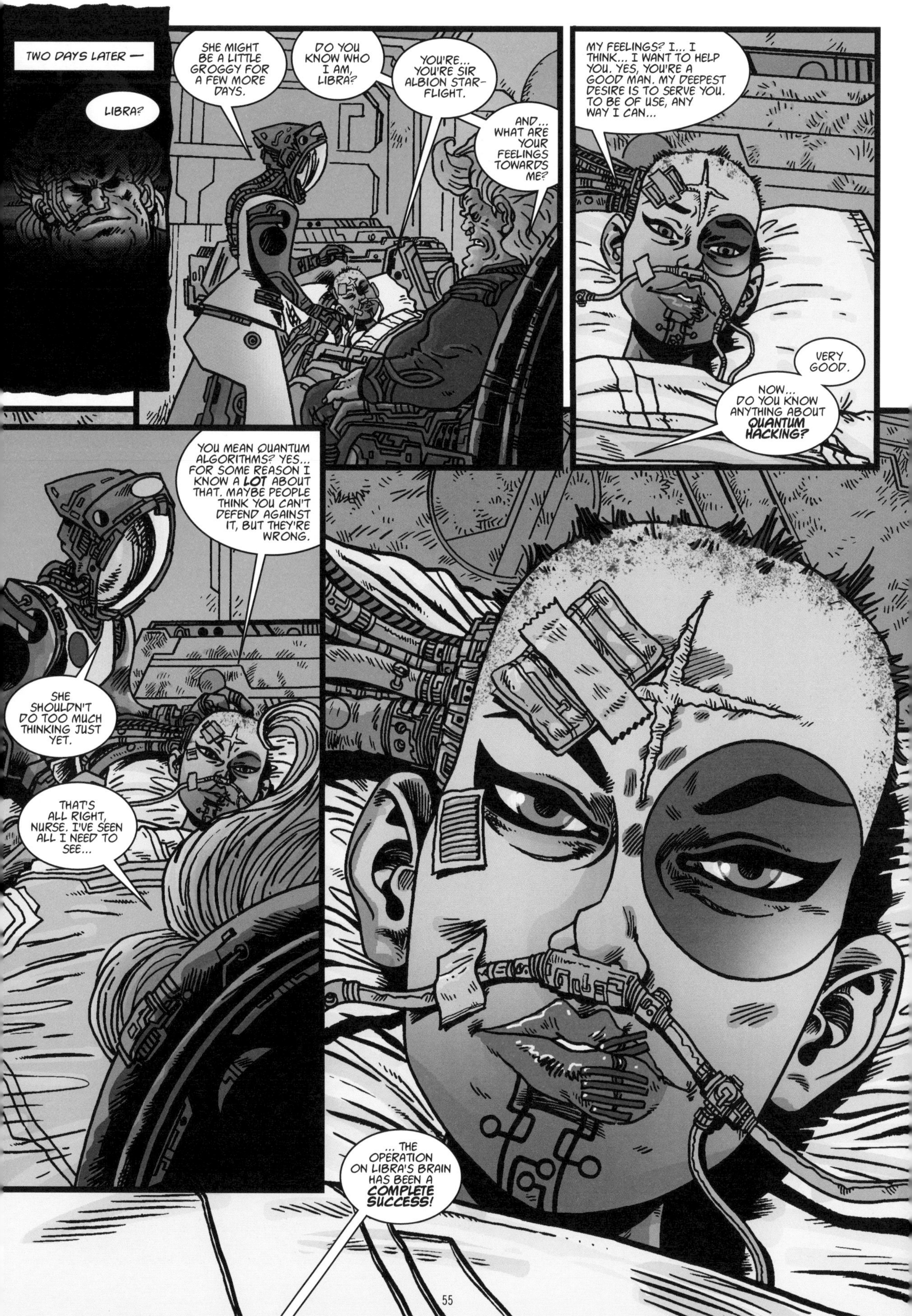
TWO DAYS LATER —
LIBRA?
SHE MIGHT BE A LITTLE GROGGY FOR A FEW MORE DAYS.
DO YOU KNOW WHO I AM, LIBRA?
YOU'RE... YOU'RE SIR ALBION STAR-FLIGHT.
AND... WHAT ARE YOUR FEELINGS TOWARDS ME?
MY FEELINGS? I... I THINK... I WANT TO HELP YOU. YES, YOU'RE A GOOD MAN. MY DEEPEST DESIRE IS TO SERVE YOU. TO BE OF USE, ANY WAY I CAN...
VERY GOOD.
NOW... DO YOU KNOW ANYTHING ABOUT QUANTUM HACKING?
YOU MEAN QUANTUM ALGORITHMS? YES... FOR SOME REASON I KNOW A LOT ABOUT THAT. MAYBE PEOPLE THINK YOU CAN'T DEFEND AGAINST IT, BUT THEY'RE WRONG.
SHE SHOULDN'T DO TOO MUCH THINKING JUST YET.
THAT'S ALL RIGHT, NURSE. I'VE SEEN ALL I NEED TO SEE...
... THE OPERATION ON LIBRA'S BRAIN HAS BEEN A COMPLETE SUCCESS!

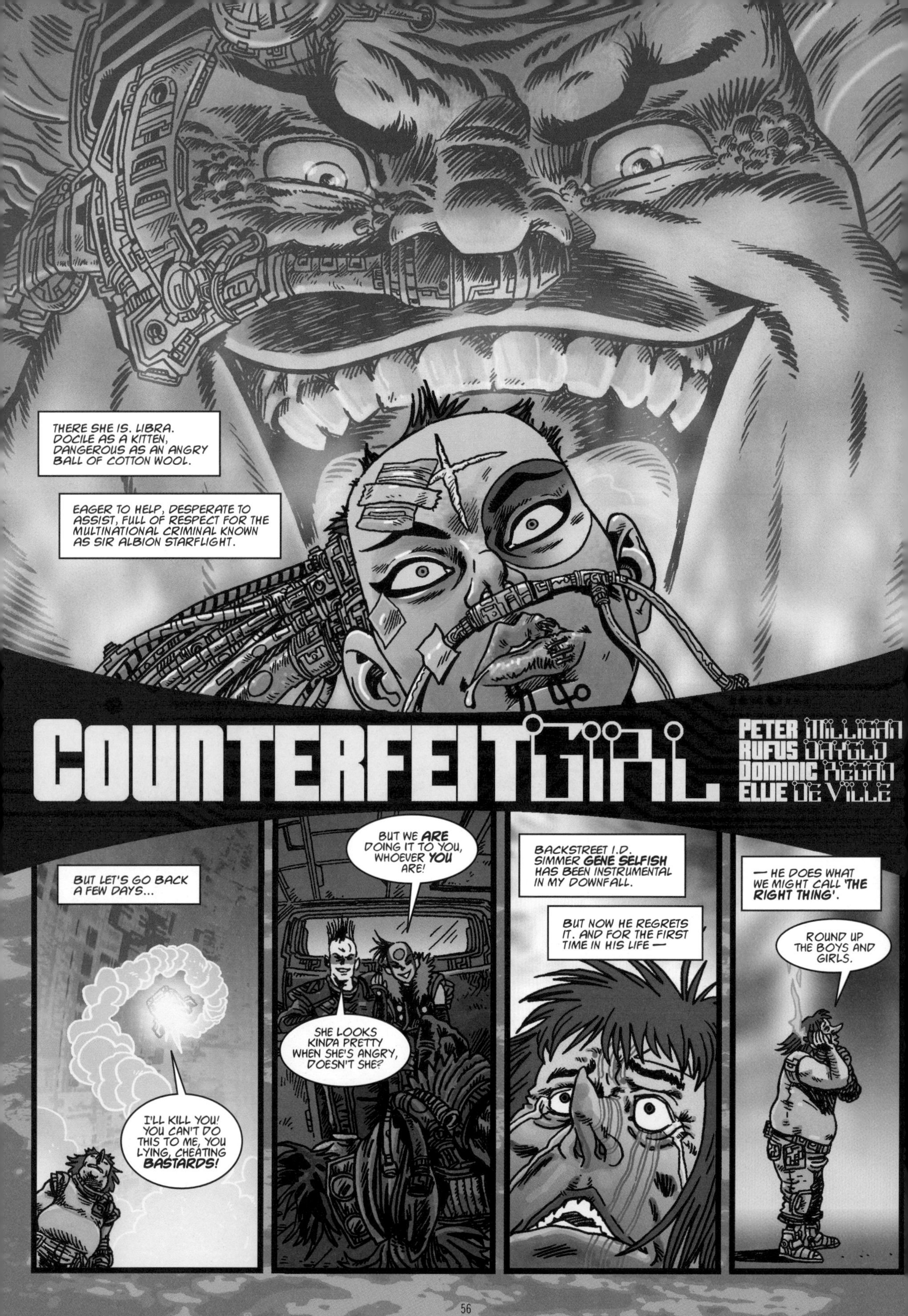

THERE SHE IS. LIBRA. DOCILE AS A KITTEN, DANGEROUS AS AN ANGRY BALL OF COTTON WOOL.
EAGER TO HELP, DESPERATE TO ASSIST, FULL OF RESPECT FOR THE MULTINATIONAL CRIMINAL KNOWN AS SIR ALBION STARFLIGHT.
COUNTERFEIT GIRL
PETER MILLIGAN
RUFUS DAYGLO
DOMINIC REGAN
ELLIE DE VILLE
BUT LET'S GO BACK A FEW DAYS...
I'LL KILL YOU! YOU CAN'T DO THIS TO ME, YOU LYING, CHEATING BASTARDS!
BUT WE ARE DOING IT TO YOU, WHOEVER YOU ARE!
SHE LOOKS KINDA PRETTY WHEN SHE'S ANGRY, DOESN'T SHE?
BACKSTREET I.D. SIMMER GENE SELFISH HAS BEEN INSTRUMENTAL IN MY DOWNFALL.
BUT NOW HE REGRETS IT. AND FOR THE FIRST TIME IN HIS LIFE —
— HE DOES WHAT WE MIGHT CALL 'THE RIGHT THING'.
ROUND UP THE BOYS AND GIRLS.

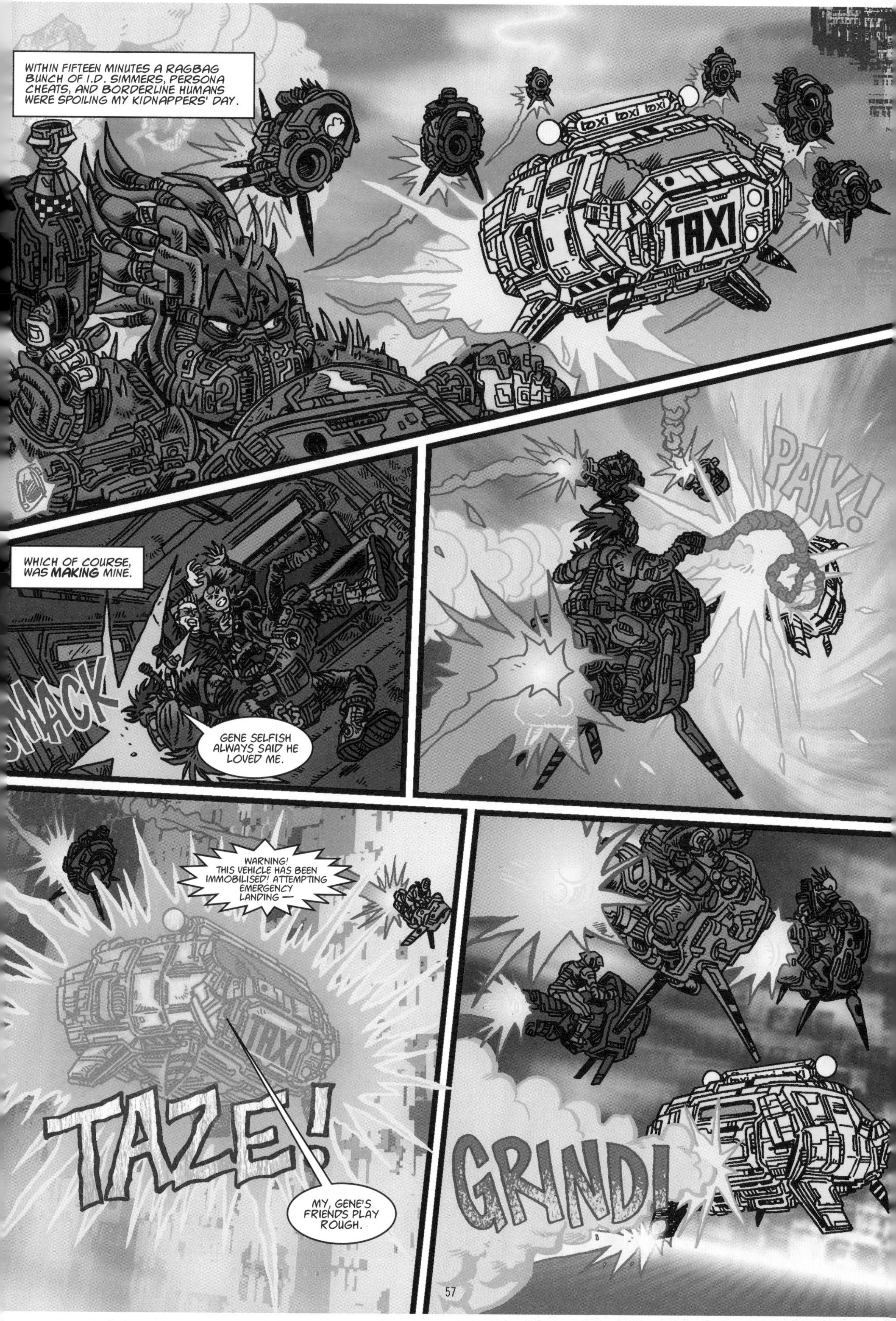
WITHIN FIFTEEN MINUTES A RAGBAG BUNCH OF I.D. SIMMERS, PERSONA CHEATS, AND BORDERLINE HUMANS WERE SPOILING MY KIDNAPPERS' DAY.
taxi taxi taxi
TAXI
WHICH OF COURSE, WAS **MAKING** MINE.
SMACK
GENE SELFISH ALWAYS SAID HE LOVED ME.
PAK!
WARNING! THIS VEHICLE HAS BEEN IMMOBILISED! ATTEMPTING EMERGENCY LANDING —
TAXI
TAZE!
MY, GENE'S FRIENDS PLAY ROUGH.
GRIND!

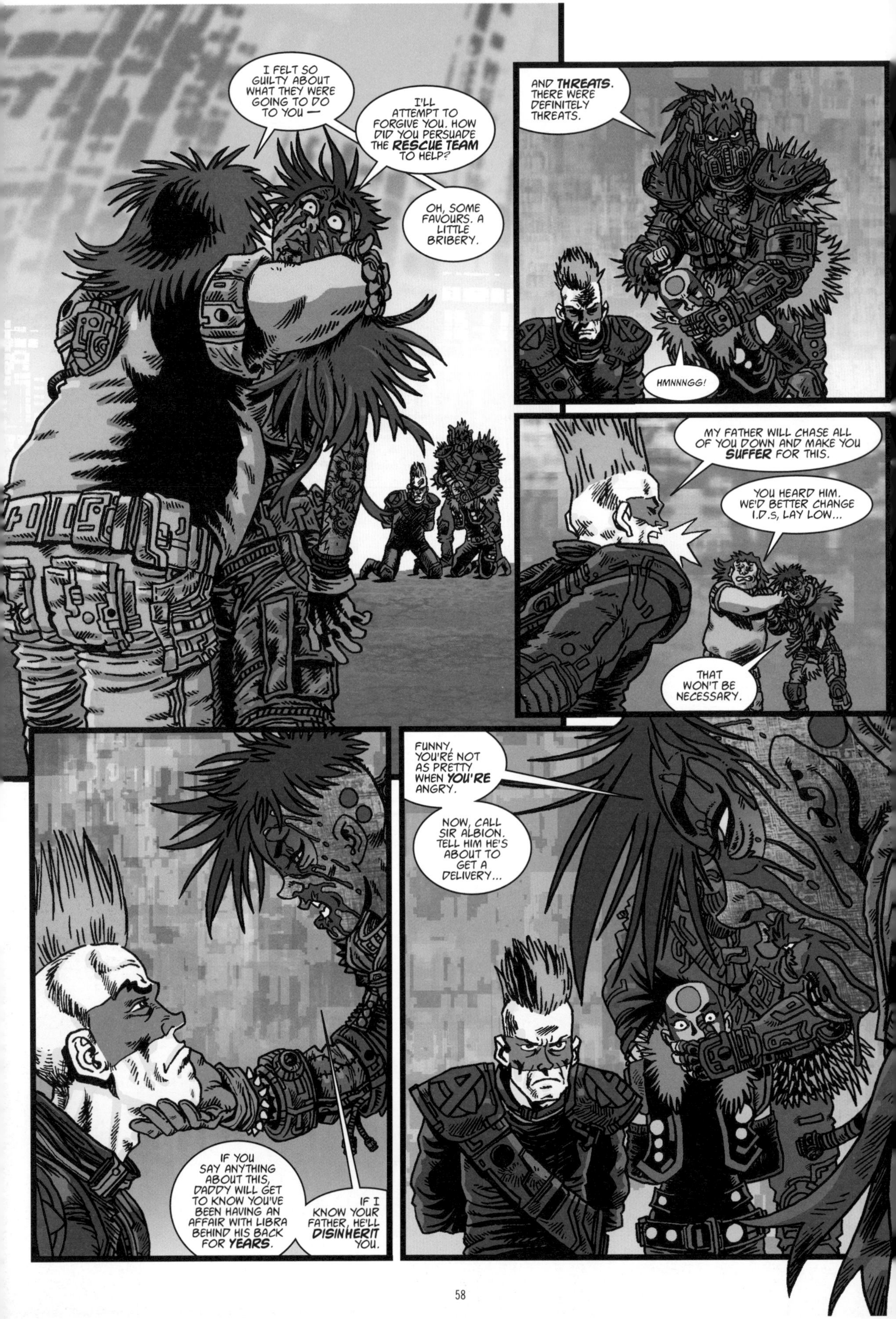

I FELT SO GUILTY ABOUT WHAT THEY WERE GOING TO DO TO YOU —
I'LL ATTEMPT TO FORGIVE YOU. HOW DID YOU PERSUADE THE **RESCUE TEAM** TO HELP?
OH, SOME FAVOURS. A LITTLE BRIBERY.
AND **THREATS**. THERE WERE DEFINITELY THREATS.
HMNNNGG!
MY FATHER WILL CHASE ALL OF YOU DOWN AND MAKE YOU **SUFFER** FOR THIS.
YOU HEARD HIM. WE'D BETTER CHANGE I.D.S, LAY LOW...
THAT WON'T BE NECESSARY.
IF YOU SAY ANYTHING ABOUT THIS, DADDY WILL GET TO KNOW YOU'VE BEEN HAVING AN AFFAIR WITH LIBRA BEHIND HIS BACK FOR **YEARS**.
IF I KNOW YOUR FATHER, HE'LL **DISINHERIT** YOU.
FUNNY, YOU'RE NOT AS PRETTY WHEN **YOU'RE** ANGRY.
NOW, CALL SIR ALBION. TELL HIM HE'S ABOUT TO GET A DELIVERY...

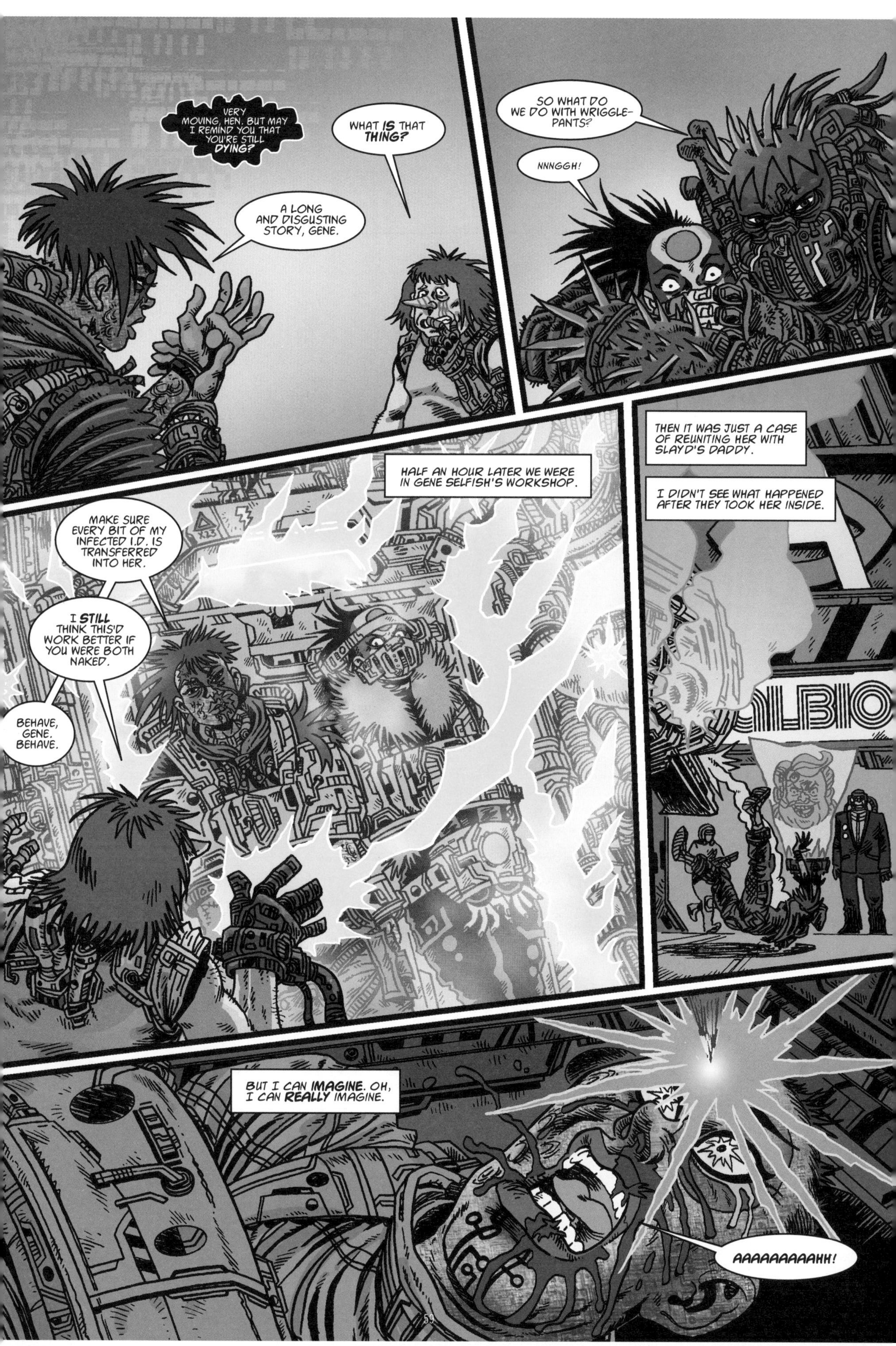

VERY MOVING, HEN. BUT MAY I REMIND YOU THAT YOU'RE STILL DYING?
WHAT IS THAT THING?
A LONG AND DISGUSTING STORY, GENE.
SO WHAT DO WE DO WITH WRIGGLE-PANTS?
NNNGGH!
HALF AN HOUR LATER WE WERE IN GENE SELFISH'S WORKSHOP.
MAKE SURE EVERY BIT OF MY INFECTED I.D. IS TRANSFERRED INTO HER.
I STILL THINK THIS'D WORK BETTER IF YOU WERE BOTH NAKED.
BEHAVE, GENE. BEHAVE.
THEN IT WAS JUST A CASE OF REUNITING HER WITH SLAYD'S DADDY.
I DIDN'T SEE WHAT HAPPENED AFTER THEY TOOK HER INSIDE.
ALBIO
BUT I CAN IMAGINE. OH, I CAN REALLY IMAGINE.
AAAAAAAAAHH!

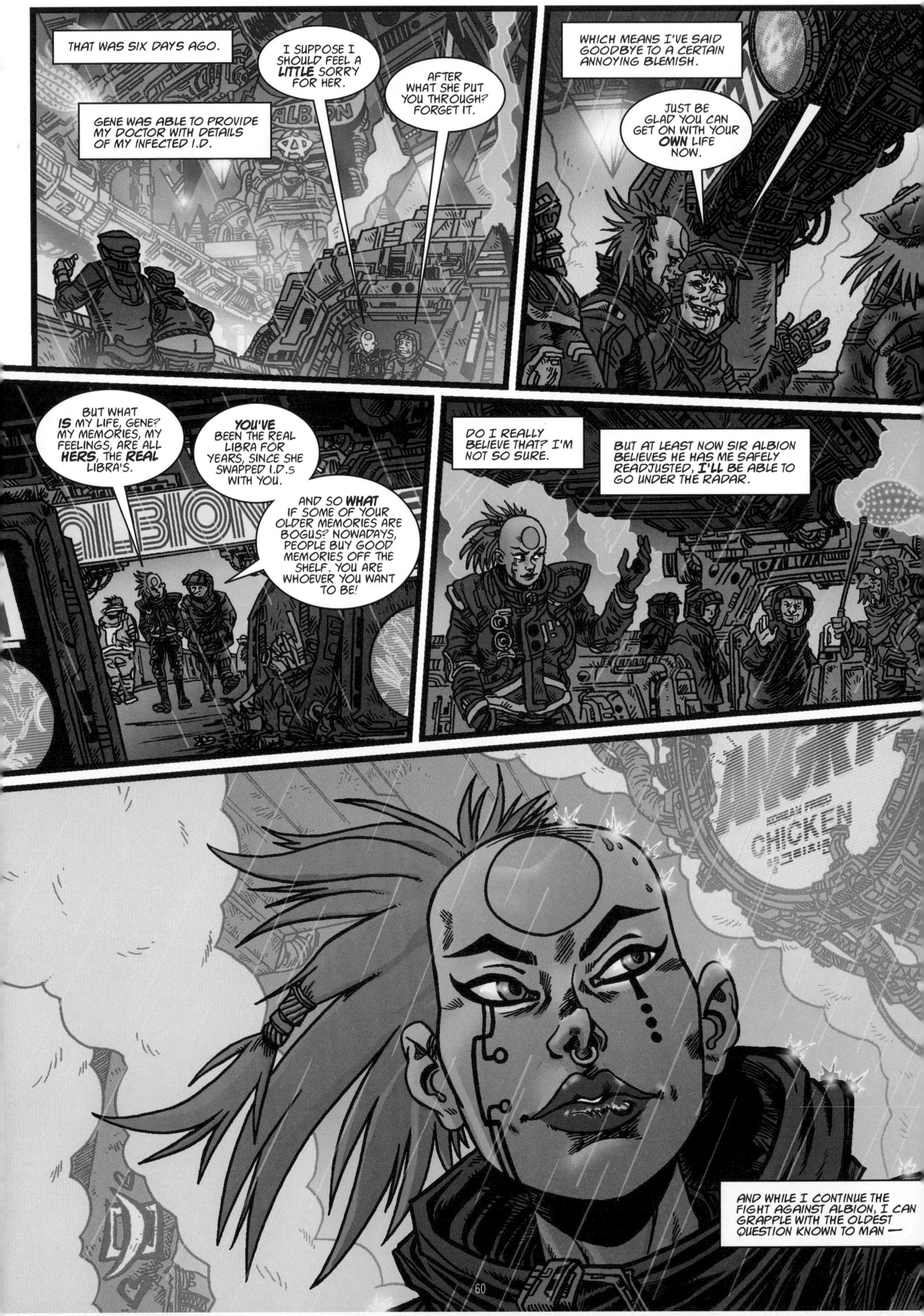

THAT WAS SIX DAYS AGO.
GENE WAS ABLE TO PROVIDE MY DOCTOR WITH DETAILS OF MY INFECTED I.D.
I SUPPOSE I SHOULD FEEL A **LITTLE** SORRY FOR HER.
AFTER WHAT SHE PUT YOU THROUGH? FORGET IT.
ALBION
WHICH MEANS I'VE SAID GOODBYE TO A CERTAIN ANNOYING BLEMISH.
JUST BE GLAD YOU CAN GET ON WITH YOUR **OWN** LIFE NOW.
BUT WHAT **IS** MY LIFE, GENE? MY MEMORIES, MY FEELINGS, ARE ALL **HERS**, THE **REAL** LIBRA'S.
YOU'VE BEEN THE REAL LIBRA FOR YEARS, SINCE SHE SWAPPED I.D.S WITH YOU.
AND SO **WHAT** IF SOME OF YOUR OLDER MEMORIES ARE BOGUS? NOWADAYS, PEOPLE BUY GOOD MEMORIES OFF THE SHELF. YOU ARE WHOEVER YOU WANT TO BE!
ALBION
DO I REALLY BELIEVE THAT? I'M NOT SO SURE.
BUT AT LEAST NOW SIR ALBION BELIEVES HE HAS ME SAFELY READJUSTED, **I'LL** BE ABLE TO GO UNDER THE RADAR.
CHICKEN
AND WHILE I CONTINUE THE FIGHT AGAINST ALBION, I CAN GRAPPLE WITH THE OLDEST QUESTION KNOWN TO MAN —

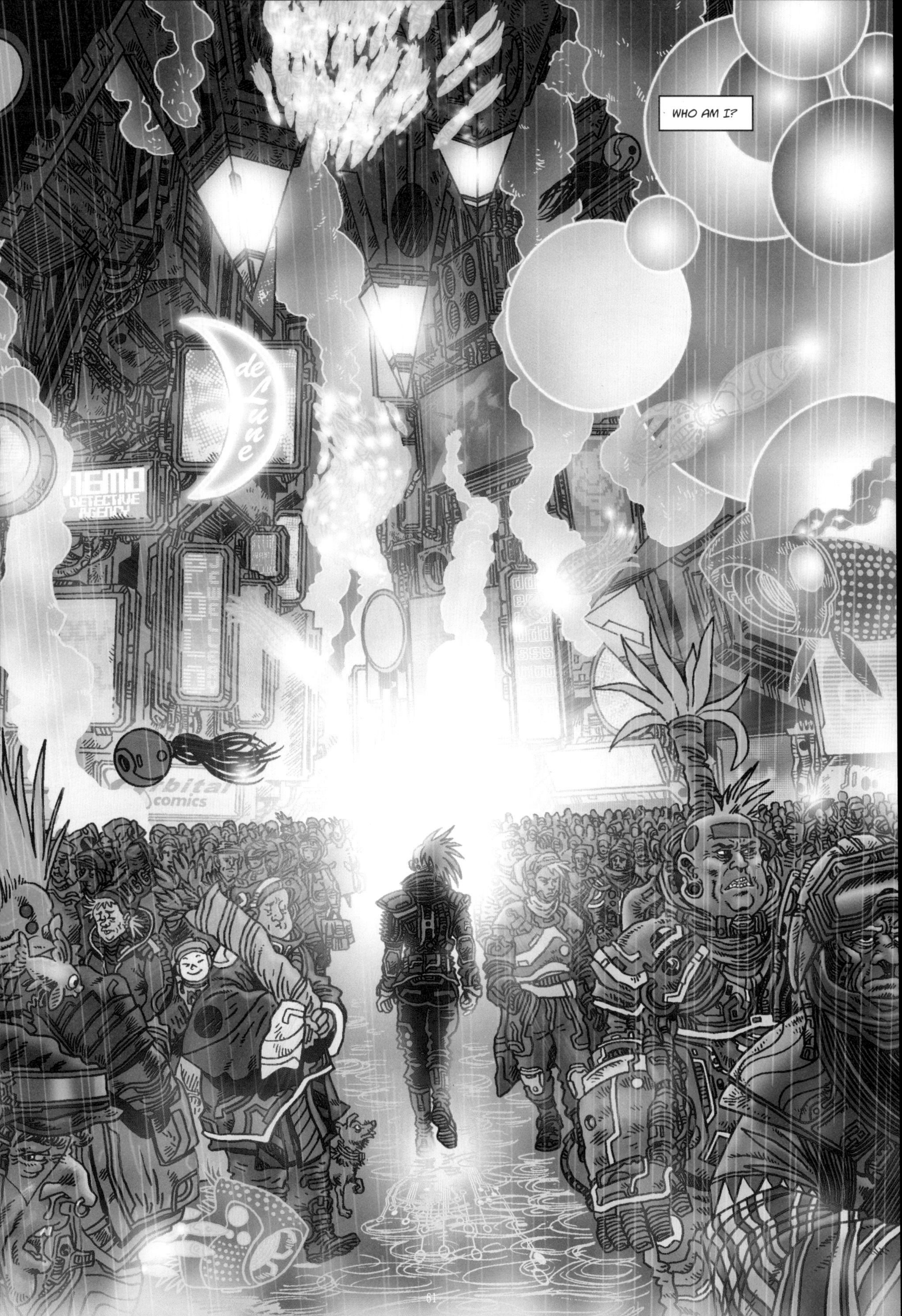
WHO AM I?
de Lune
NEMO
DETECTIVE AGENCY
comics

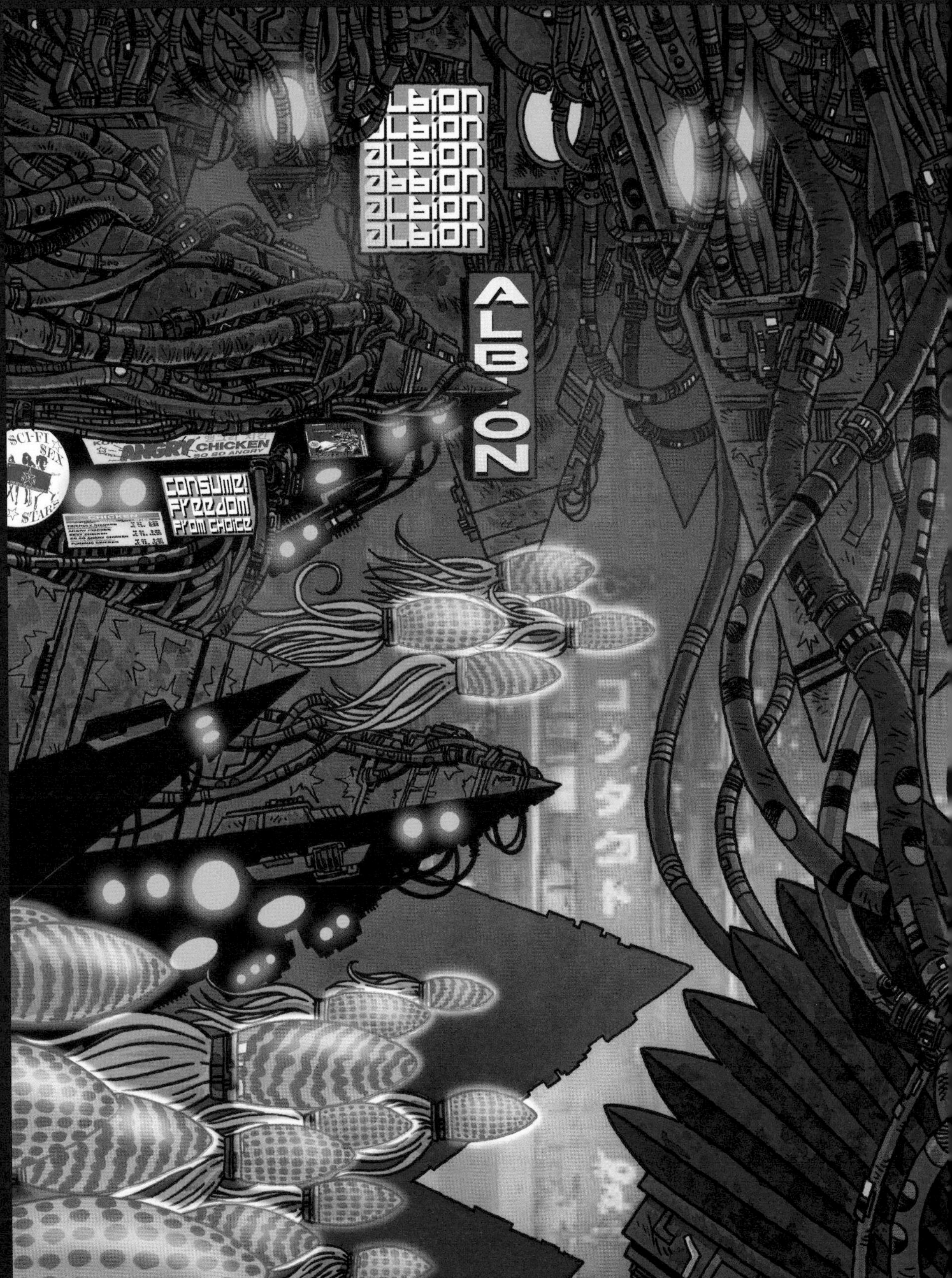
ALBION
ALBION
ALBION
ALBION
ALBION
ALBION
ALBION
SCI-FI SEX STARS
ANGRY CHICKEN
SO SO ANGRY
CONSUME! FREEDOM FROM CHOICE
コンタクト

Cover by **Rufus Dayglo**

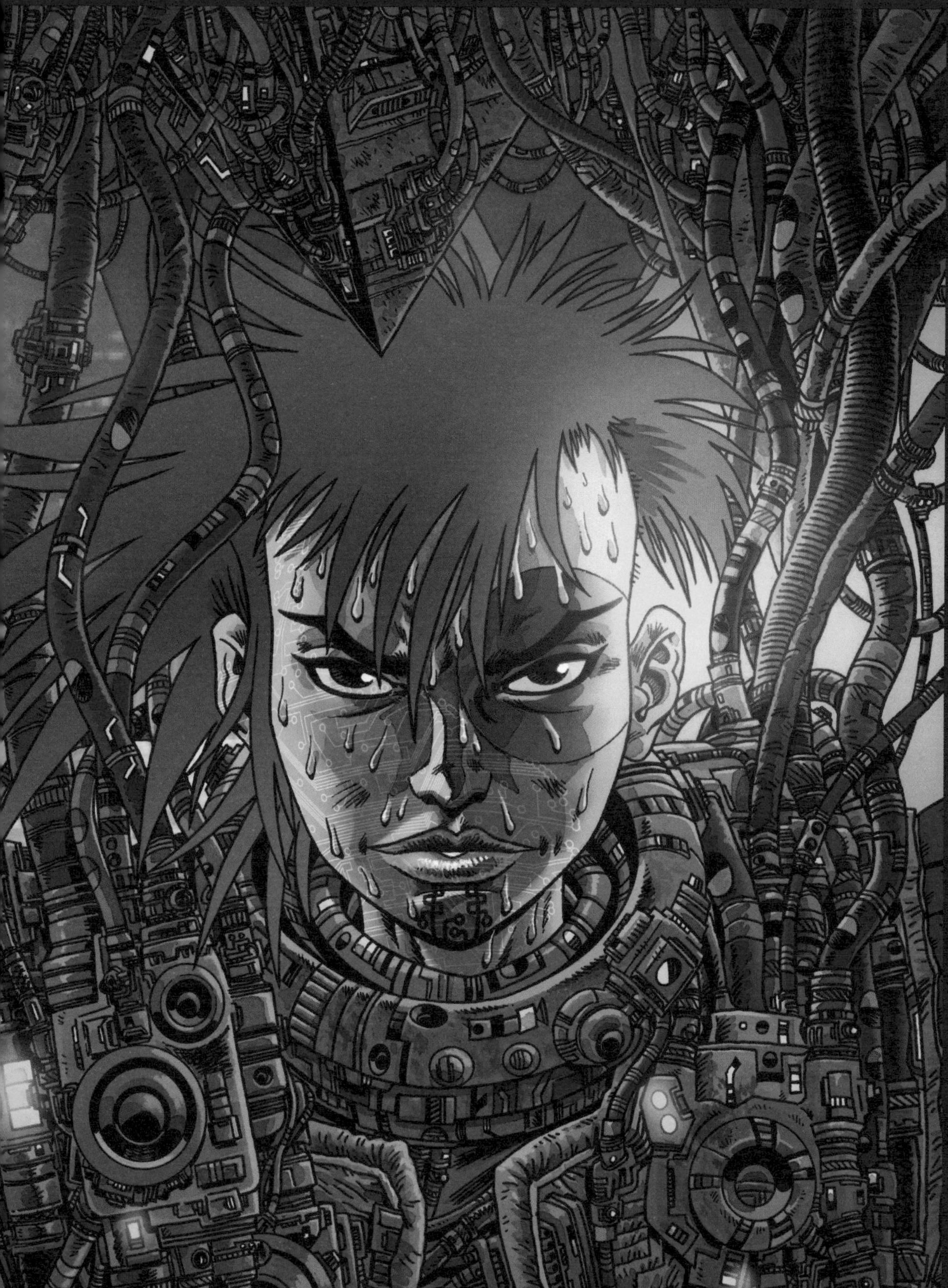

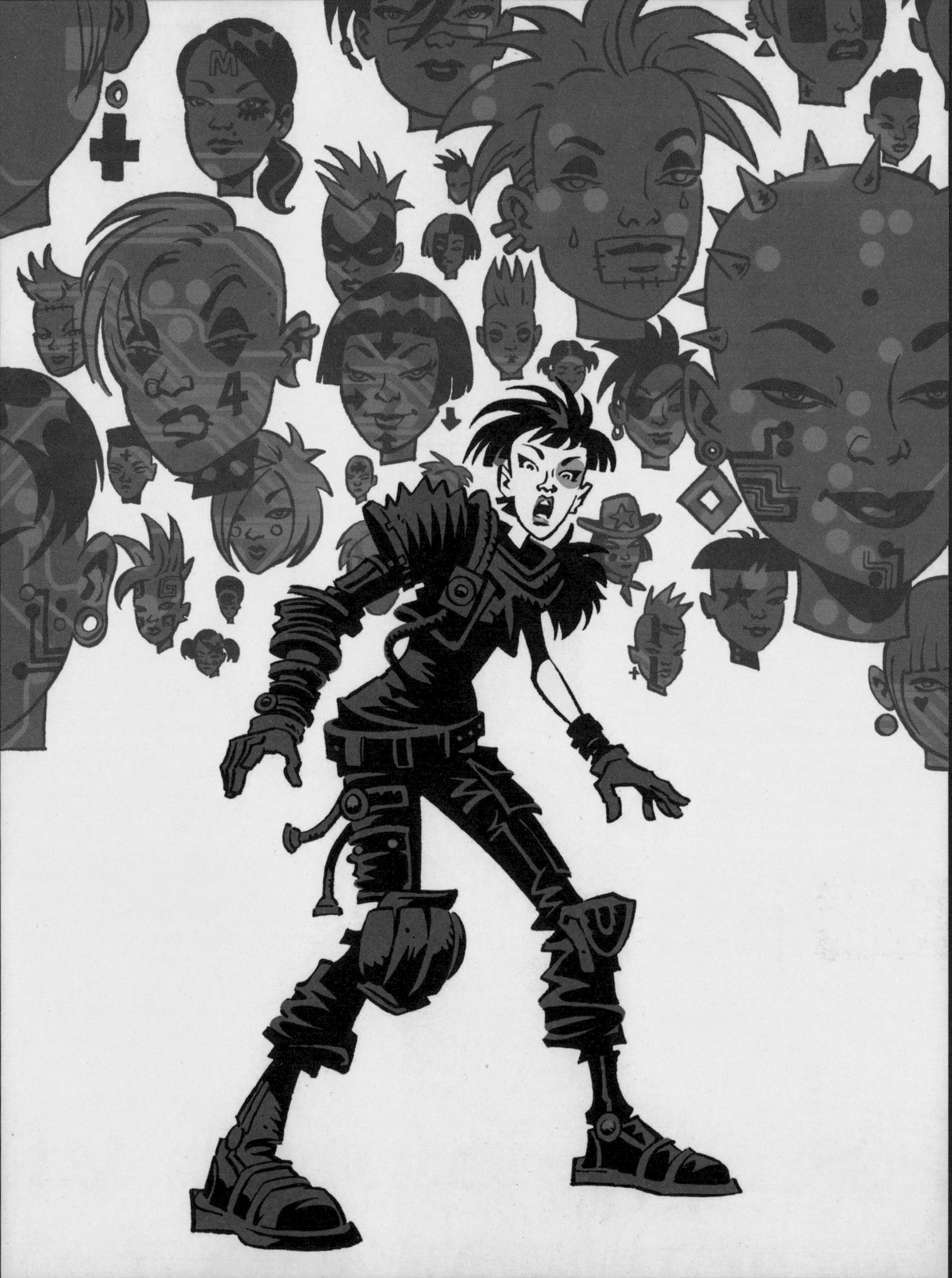